SUPER STAYING POWER

What You Need to Become Valuable and Resilient at Work!

JASON SEIDEN

Mc
Graw
Hill

New York   Chicago   San Francisco   Lisbon   London   Madrid   Mexico City
Milan   New Delhi   San Juan   Seoul   Singapore   Sydney   Toronto

Library of Congress Cataloging-in-Publication Data

Seiden, Jason.
   Super staying power : what you need to become valuable and resilient at work / Jason
Seiden.
       p.   cm.
   Includes index.
   ISBN 978-0-07-163716-9
       1. Employee motivation.   2. Employees—Psychology.   3. Work—Psychological
aspects.   4. Success in business.   I. Title.

   HF5549.5.M63S45   2010
   650.1—dc22   2009028528

1 2 3 4 5 6 7 8 9 10 11 12 13 14 15 16 17 18 19 20 21 22 23   FGR/FGR   0 9

ISBN 978-0-07-163716-9
MHID   0-07-163716-8

Interior design by Think Book Works

McGraw-Hill books are available at special quantity discounts to use as premiums and sales
promotions or for use in corporate training programs. To contact a representative, please e-mail
us at bulksales@mcgraw-hill.com.

*Styra, I know you still whisper
encouragement to me when you can.
Thank you for everything.
I love you and miss you.*

Contents

PART 1

Seeing Success in a Magic Moment

CHAPTER 1 Magic Moments

CHAPTER 2 A Goal You Can Commit To

PART 2

Reinforcing the Winner's Attitude Through the Three Perspectives   81

Foreword

Wisdom is not gained from a book but from the discussions that surround it. Following is a part of one such discussion, in which executives, students, psychologists, human resources practitioners, attorneys, bloggers, managers, job seekers, business owners, account executives, sales professionals, and financial advisors, from Korea to London to Brazil to Philadelphia, have taken part.

Career resiliency is . . .

". . . 'having a pulse for today and your heart beat for tomorrow.'
We need to keep a pulse on the business and drivers today while
we create an exciting vision for tomorrow."
   —Kristen Richardson, global human resources executive

". . . knowing how to recognize opportunities when they present themselves. I chuckle sometimes when I hear young people,
especially undergrads, talk about an entire career trajectory as if
it's preordained. I say this to them: 'Pay attention to the buffeting winds.'"
   —Frank Roche, employee communications expert

". . . having your priorities in order. Knowing your goals. Having
character. Behaving with integrity. Those people who crumble
easily? They need to work on their own personal infrastruture."
   —Laurie Ruettimann, human resources blogger

". . . positive persistence toward what you want—persistence despite all the naysayers."

                              —Angela Jacobs, workforce architect

". . . accepting criticism and responding to the critique. Being prepared to fail and learning how not to repeat the mistake."

                              —Adam Greetis, attorney

". . . the mental state of being open to change, understanding change, and seeing options within change."

                              —Paul Hebert, managing director

". . . tolerance of uncertainty, adaptability, a big network, and lots of outlets for your frustrations."   —Rohit Talwar, futurist

". . . knowing the right people . . . and not being afraid to ask for help."   —Michael Shvartsman, recent college graduate

". . . the ability to adapt and change in a dynamic environment without losing focus on what's important."

                              —Virginia Venable, consultant

". . . being a *voracious* learner about social media."

                              —Ken Moir, human resources professional

". . . owning up to reality."

                              —Ryan Cooke, industrial organizational psychologist

What happens when you join the chorus? Find out: explore alternative views on career resiliency, expand your network, and contribute your own ideas to the common genius at http://jasonseiden.com/superstayingpower.

Acknowledgments

I am lucky for many reasons, chief among them being my great fortune to have had a string of truly stellar teachers. The lessons I learned from them are never far from my mind, and I want to acknowledge several of the standouts: Paul Grant, John Nickel, Tim Conway, Joyce Witt, Sally Schwartz, Todd Metz, and Ed Ruda. Even among this group, a few merit special mention:

Mr. Grant, you are the first among peers on this list. Your classroom was magic, and the love for learning you drew out from me guides me to this day. I joke with friends that I peaked shortly after fourth grade and have been on a downward slide ever since. I have made my mission in life to protect the magic you instilled within us and share it with others. Your impact extends far beyond those you had in class . . . and I think I speak for almost everyone from our Red Oak class of '83 when I say, "Thank God it does."

Todd, with laughter, realism, and unmatched power of spirit, you showed me how to make pressure disappear, under extreme conditions and zero margin of error. Though I didn't have the words for them then, your lessons gave rise to my philosophies of "more perfect" and "active adaptation." Thank you.

Ed, your classroom covers every aspect of life. I owe you a great deal, yet rarely have I expressed my gratitude for what you have done for me. I have learned more about myself through you than any other person I have known, bar none. For permission to use your wisdom as the backbone of this book, for helping turn my formal education into meaningful expertise, for my favorite person on the planet, and for everything I have learned from you, thank you. When I think of the giants whose shoulders I am perched upon—and rest assured, I am under no illusion that I got here alone—you are one of the first.

I also want to acknowledge the teachers I have been lucky enough to have at home. Dad, Mom, Lori, Jeff, Jackie, Alexis . . . I'm a published author and I'm bringing up the rear in my own family. And that's OK with me; I draw inspiration from each of you. Then there's Elle and Jaz and Vanessa, all living proof that I am the luckiest man on the planet, and without whom . . . without whom . . . you know, I have no idea how to finish that sentence. I hope I never learn. (V, yer stuck with me, babe. I love you. Always have, always will.)

And last but not least, I need to acknowledge two people without whom this book simply would not exist. Laurie Ruettimann, who went out of her way to help broker this deal, and Michele Wells, who decided to take a chance on an unknown and worked under an insane deadline to turn my raw material into something truly great. Michele, this book is a significant Magic Moment in my life. Thank you.

Introduction

> **IN THIS SECTION**
>
> ▶ Why do so many people struggle to define career success?
> ▶ What is the most important factor in determining your success?
> ▶ What is it called when we blame external factors for problems rather than acknowledge our own failure to correct for emotional currents?
> ▶ How will *Super Staying Power* help you?

Work. You do it every day.

But how well?

Well enough to know that if the axe falls, someone will be watching to take care of you, making sure you don't get let go? Well enough that if the top manager leaves, she'll pick you to join her at the new company? Well enough that when recruiters come asking about who the real driver of the operations is, it's your name they'll get? Well enough that if the company "explodes," you'll have people watching for you in the wings, falling over themselves to scoop you up?

Let me back up: do you even know what doing your job "well" means?

Do you understand what it takes to build a career with staying power? Do you think it means doing what your boss asks? Do you think it means getting on the glamorous projects, grabbing the credit for what goes right, and constantly polishing your personal brand? Do you think all success is luck and it's your duty to suffer in silence until the day someone worthy deigns to promote you? Or maybe you think

1

that politics and backstabbing are the only paths to success, or that the proverbial "better mousetrap" will always win out in the end?

Most people have no idea what it takes to be successful. Here's a hint: done right, it's the kind of hard work you don't mind doing. It's rewarding, it's simple, and it's controlled by nobody but yourself.

It's also probably not what you're thinking.

Today's Popular Models Are Broken

The model for what success looks like in the real world has been crowded out by countless stylized, satirized, or patently false versions that have been created by others—others who used their customized versions of success to sell you entertainment, or art, or a path to success just like theirs that may or may not work for you. Let's look at four frameworks people use to understand work, and the problems with each.

TV Shows and Movies

In TV office settings, either humor or drama is purposefully amplified. Why? Because real life frequently includes long stretches of boredom, and watching television and movies is our escape from those boring stretches. When we're bored, we want to be entertained by stories that are more engaging and funnier than our own day-to-day experiences. On TV, I want to see affairs, revenge, and stupidity on a scale impossible in an overmedicated real world. Actually, *I* don't want to see any of that, but apparently lots of other people do.

Movies operate the same way as television, only more so, unless it's an action flick, in which case office scenes are washed out in order to make the chase sequences "pop."

If you're not a storyteller, you don't pay attention to the formula. After a while, you forget that what you're watching has been manipulated in order to tell a particular story. You forget it's not the real thing. Sure, in your head you know it's not real, but our brains are lazy, and after too much exposure to manipulated storylines, our brains get tired of storing the fake stuff apart from the real stuff, and our memories of TV show plotlines and our memories of what happened to us four jobs back start to get mingled. At this point, our expectations of others change, we lose our sense of empathy, and our capacity for critical thinking is diminished, because we start to expect real life to look like what we see on our screens.

Then one day it dawns on us: we're not moving up the ladder, the call from Morpheus we've been waiting for isn't ever going to come, and we have no idea what to do next.

The News

News, like TV, sells drama. It has to; ad rates are determined by how many eyeballs are watching, which means news programs compete not only with other news programs but also with everything else on the tube vying for our attention at a given moment. News producers use the same storytelling tricks as everyone else: overdramatized backgrounds, exaggerated headlines, and sensational storylines are just part of the repertoire.

This leads to business stories with a proven ability to hook viewers . . . but after so many tales of what Millennials wear to work, criminal CEOs, and the overworked middle class, lazy brains stop discounting stories for their sensational factor and begin to accept what's being said at face value.

Do you remember what the big news story was during the summer of 2001? It was about shark attacks off the Gulf Coast of Florida. It seemed like all they talked about until September. I had never seen such intense news coverage on the topic before, and I haven't heard a thing about it since then. What, had there never been a shark attack before? Has there not been one since?

Just because the news stations report something doesn't make it relevant. It simply means that a producer believes the story is sensational enough to drive up viewership. But when you don't think critically about the stories you're told, you begin to interpret your world through this filter provided by the news outlets. You lose your perspective about what's really going on in the world without even realizing it. As far as you know, sharks left the Florida coast for good after September 10, 2001. It's like letting someone slip a magnet under your personal compass: the device still reads "north," but who knows what direction you're really heading!

School

School is wonderful, isn't it? So neat and tidy, with standardized performance measures, bell curves, and an answer to the question, "Will this be on the test?" There's just one problem: life's not so tidy. Companies, unlike students, can change the game in order to secure a better "grade." Coworkers can, too. But we don't even need to go there; we can look at a simple career progression to see the problem with the school mentality in the business world.

Start with "Jane Allayes." She was a straight A student who got hired into MegaCorp's management training program. She knocks the cover off the ball—really impresses her manager—and quickly gets promoted. Again, she impresses her manager and is bumped forward. And so on, until Jane is made CEO. That's the day Jane wakes up, looks around, and freaks out because there is no one to give her a meaningful grade. If she plays to the shareholders, she'll overemphasize short-term financial results. If she plays to the board of directors, she'll get caught up in politics. If she plays to management, she'll have put the foxes in charge of the hen house. As CEO, Jane needs to display the ability to handle ambiguity, and that's the one thing school never taught her to do well. Sorry, Jane, you were well prepped to get the job, but no one prepped you to actually *do* it.

Jane's face will soon be all over the news . . . in a shocking story asking why a person with such stellar credentials could have ever turned out to be such an incompetent, unethical CEO.

(Actually, Jane never makes it to CEO. She'll blame the "glass ceiling," but the problem is really something different. We'll dive into this issue a bit later.)

The Law of Attraction

The law of attraction is a great concept, and very popular lately. One small problem: the way it's being packaged today is often indistinguishable from "wishful thinking." Without loud calls for hard work, progress feedback, continual balancing between adaptation and perseverance, active management of environmental factors, and crystallization of one's awareness of one's own mental derailers, it's snake oil. I might as well hand you the blueprints for a skyscraper and tell you the penthouse apartment is yours—all you need to do is to build the building. Don't look at me like that, I gave you the blueprints! Follow my design exactly, and it'll be there, waiting for you!

Mental Models

And that's the problem: your primary mental models about how work is supposed to look are off. They are not calibrated with reality. If they ever were, once upon a time, they have since been de-calibrated from reality by the TV shows you watch, by the movies you enjoy, by your schooling, by the self-help books you read. (Not this one, of course.) These stylized models, once held separate in your mind from the realistic ones, get all mixed up in time.

By contrast, if you grew up playing Little League, your mental model for baseball is probably near perfect. And why shouldn't it be? Unlike work, which you've been doing for only a short while, you've been playing baseball your whole life. Even if you haven't played in years, you likely still know all the important rules of the game.

For instance, raise your hand if you know how many outs per side in an inning. That's a pretty basic rule. You should all know it. (Unless you grew up playing cricket, in which case you're off the hook.) You may even know more advanced rules, like the infield fly rule, too. I could drop you on a diamond with seventeen other former Little Leaguers, and y'all could find positions and start playing without a problem. In fact, I bet I could dump you on a diamond with five others, and chances are you could pretty quickly negotiate a revised set of rules that still let you play a game pretty close to the real thing. (Hint: your childhood is here, and it brought "imaginary runners.")

By this stage of life, you know more than just the rules. You know game strategy, too. You know simple things like "calling" the ball as an outfielder to avoid collisions, and more advanced things like when to sprint straight at first base and when to round it in anticipation of a possible double. You may even know more subtle strategies about when to rest a pitcher or how to pick a team.

You know all this because every time you played, watched, or talked about baseball, your mental model was a faithful representation of the real thing.

Preventative Wisdom for Work

At the risk of repeating myself: most people's mental pictures of work are nowhere close to the real thing. I know this because I've seen them at it, and they're a mess. And I don't care if they work in corner offices, cubes, or coffee shops. It doesn't matter if we're talking about entrepreneurs or corporate drones. They could be in sales or engineering. Whatever.

Now, some of you might be out there reading this right now, jumping up and down, thinking, *Yes! I mean, my perception of work reality is perfect, but the people I work with . . . well, let's just say I've been preaching this stuff for years and they still don't get it!* The good news is this book can help them. The other good news is this book can help you, too, because while you see yourself as an island of at-least-someone-gets-it-iveness, half a century of scientific study tells us that people like you (and me, and your coworkers in contracts, and all of us) tend to overestimate our abilities. By a lot. No worries, though; by the time you're done reading *Super Staying Power*—provided you pay attention and put these concepts into action as you go—you'll be every bit as good as you think you are now.

There are also probably some of you who can't understand why this book is necessary. You think, *"Wow, all those little Millenni-*

als working for me should already know this! If they'd just put down the computers and YouTubes and X Things and do what they're supposed to do, I could retire in two years like I planned, instead of ten." (Assuming retirement is still an option at all.) Ah, what wonderful self-awareness.

And finally, a few of you may be squirming in your seats. Maybe you read my blog or you've seen me speak, and you can see where this is going and you know you're about to get thumped right between the eyes. It's OK. You're not the first to need help: in applying ourselves to business—and for that matter, religion, nation building, war fighting, peace making, city planning, and family raising, just to name a few other things we've applied ourselves to over the years—mankind has been making mistakes since the dawn of time. So you're in good company.

At the heart of the matter is the fact that many people—wherever they work, whatever they do—lack any real sense of what work is. They may have watched Dad or Mom go to work in the morning and come home late, but they never really asked about what went on while their parents were gone. They just looked at the tired expression on their parents' faces at the end of the day, decided they "didn't want to be like that when they grew up," and plugged the headphones back in.

These folks are now working, and they don't know what they're supposed to be doing. They don't know who they should be talking to, or how conversations are supposed to sound. They have never seen real work, only dramatized, sensationalized versions of it. They're oblivious to how most of the things they do scream "Rookie!" to the outside world . . . so they go about their days, getting mad at the world for not giving them a fair shot, only occasionally asking themselves, "What is it about me that makes so many people think they can see through me? Am I doing something wrong? Or are they just being unfair?"

Now, I'm a firm believer that the world has got to change and that the world of tomorrow will—and should!—look vastly different from the world of today. But at the same time, I have no desire to throw the good out with the bad. Every generation must relearn the fundamentals of work for itself; there is, however, no law that says every generation must learn these fundamentals through experience. It is completely acceptable to learn from the experiences of others.

That's what wisdom is all about.

That's what this book is all about.

A Note to the Next Generation

Are you really history in the making? As they say, "If the shoe fits . . ."

Breaking newsflash: I'm a Gen Xer. And whoever *you* are, I'm one of the people who want you to win. Along with a few million of my peers, I've either supported you or blazed a trail for you, acting as a Sherpa and lugging all this gear up so you could reach the summit. The glory is yours—go for it!

I love my role. I occupy a very special place in history, bridging two giant generations. And I happen to be a good bridge—I feel like I was put on this earth specifically to help everyone transition from the old to the new. I have a natural knack for transitions, a passion for facilitating, and the training to do it well. Someone once commented that I like to bring structure to chaos, and I had to correct her: Sherpas don't bring structure to chaos. The team does that. I bring the tools. I lay the ladders and ropes out to make the mountain more manageable. *You* do the real work.

Here we stand at base camp, ready to depart, and I'm looking at my up-and-coming peers—the ones who are not yet jaded, who still have both potential and hope—and I can almost hear you thinking about how older generations are bitter because destiny has chosen you for glory. You wish we'd end our infatuation with you and get past this whole Gen Y / Millennial / Digital Generation thing already. You've developed your own climbing technique that renders all prior knowledge obsolete . . . big deal, let's get on with it already, right? You're eager to be treated like the adults you know you are. Hell, you have all these great ideas, if we'd just listen! If we only *would* listen to your brilliance, we'd be floored with your insights! We'd be compelled to sign up to implement your ideas, and nirvana would be a short hop away. Boy, you'd make quite a collection of "idea guys," if we'd just get you the resources to execute!

The sound you're about to hear is the sound of the other shoe dropping. On your head.

You're totally oblivious. I mean, I love you, but you're nuts. Your whole sense of work is wrong, and your interpretation of your own value is wrong as a result. You're brilliant, yes, but so was every generation that came before you. Thinking the big thoughts? No shortage of smart guys have done that before you. You bring almost zero marginal value to the human race as idea guys. Executing? Now there's where you can make a difference. Because you can't just think about climbing the mountain, and you can't delegate your place in history. You yourself have to climb. And here you sit at base camp, pontificating on your significance, with your oxygen tank strapped to your backside and that magnet still stuck to the bottom of your compass. Start executing, *then* we'll listen. It's not about paying your dues; it's about demonstrating an accurate awareness of what your value is.

Now, at this point some of you may be thinking, *That Seiden guy, he sounds like a jerk. Listen to him, harshing all over my genius!*

Please, don't sell me short. I may be the biggest thorn you will ever have in your side! I'm what's stuck in your craw, and I bite, sting, and kick. I'm worse than the worst older brother. I am going to kick you in the ass and knock you in the head until I am confident that those two entities have been adequately separated, then I'm going to clean you up and push you out of the house. And I'm going to do it all with love, and in private. To the outside world, I am your biggest supporter.

Hear that, world? This "next generation"—whoever *that* is—is AWESOME. Just give them a little more understanding, OK? And don't laugh when they think no one's ever thought their brilliant thoughts, OK? They haven't discovered yet that thinking the big thoughts is easy; it's the *other* half of the battle where things are won or lost. But they'll figure it out. (You did.) They're good. They oughta be: we taught 'em! And about two hundred pages from now, they'll have mastered the concept.

Now world, this next paragraph is just for our younger peers. Please skip it. Thanks!

How old are you? Twenty-something? Thirty-something? It's time to stand on your own two feet. Look, you'll win or lose on your own terms. You'll do it your way. I get that—we all get that. But at least let's be clear on what game you intend to play. Or what mountain you intend to climb. There are no "idea guys" in this world. There are only doers.

Do Your Work Well

Follow me off the mountain and back to the baseball diamond for a moment. It's too bad you don't play ball for a living. With all the stuff you've learned about baseball, you'd maybe be somebody by now. But you don't. Instead, you work, and what you've seen from Dunder Mifflin is about as useful to your career as feathers to a fish.

What this means is, if you want to stay employed in this economy, we're going to have to deprogram you to release all the garbage expectations you have about what a job is *supposed* to be, and reprogram you for what a job *is* in the real world. We're going to have to teach you what it means to do your work well.

When we're done with our time together, you will not be the same person you are today.

You'll be much, much better.

"OK, Where Does All This Come From?"

Hi. My name is Jason Seiden. You can call me Jase. I'm your guide on this journey. There are a lot of things about me that qualify me to act as your guide, but there's really only one that matters: I can get the job done.

Let me note right up front, I'm not here to drop any new science on you. My modus operandi with *Super Staying Power* is to help you succeed using knowledge and skills you already have, theories that have already been proven, and wisdom that has been part of the human experience for ages. The world is changing pretty darn fast right now. I'll show you how to find the answers quickly from the clutter of experiences and expertise we already share. Don't be fooled: this is more than grab-and-go career development. This is applied science— a direct line from the original researchers to you, providing you with what you need to solve your problems.

If I've done my job well, this book will engage you emotionally, show you a side of success you may not have considered—but need to—and fundamentally change the way you approach your work. I genuinely believe you'll put this book down a more self-sufficient person than when you picked it up. No secrets, no pseudoscience, no sleight of hand. Just the common genius we all share, wrapped in a bit of snark and a genuine interest to see you succeed. The world needs more success stories. Let's make sure you're one of them.

I've been helping people with their jobs professionally as a consultant now for about a decade. The people I work with are no dummies; they constantly challenge me to provide real value, and if I can't help them, I don't earn a paycheck. (So far, so good.)

I have had the privilege and the pleasure to have worked for and with great people who were and are true titans in business and industry, men and women with three-letter titles at well-known companies. I basically watched, listened, and studied. Before that, I was a manager and an entrepreneur, and before that, a student of management and finance. And before that? I grew up in one of those suburbs where powerful people raise their families. I got to watch company executives at their homes before I even realized who or what they were. I understand the mind of the business owner from a lifetime of exposure to it. I understand the mind of the employee from a lifetime of exposure to that, too. Through my studies and my work, I have found a way to bridge the two. That's where this book comes from: formal study, personal experience, direct observation of success cases, and a decade of experimentation as a consultant.

That's enough about me. You can verify that I grew up in Highland Park, Illinois, went to Wharton and Kellogg for college and b-school, and have worked with real clients, online, anytime. Start with http://jasonseiden.com, where you can find everything you could want, including recommendations for my work, links to my connections (let me know who you'd like to meet), and lots and lots of content (including videos starring my bulldog, Lenny, who's very popular online).

The rest of the book now is about you.

Let the Deprogramming Begin

OK, question: Which would be the thing that would most help you succeed: More money? More time? Better skills?

Trick question.

It's not more money. That would simply amplify your current state without changing anything. It's not more time, either. If you had the power to bend time, you wouldn't be dealing with whatever issues you're presently dealing with. You'd be revered as a minor deity.

Perhaps surprisingly, it's not skills, either. In their quest to succeed at work, most people want to jump straight into skill development. They think that if they just do their job "better," all their problems will go away. They'll command more salary, they'll free up time because of their efficiency. I wrote *How to Self-Destruct: Making the Least of What's Left of Your Career* about "most people."

If you really want to win, you don't start with goals. You don't start with methodologies, systems, processes, numbers, or plans to help you understand the underlying issue, either. You start with the basics. You start with the human element.

Prepare Yourself as a Human First

Before anything else, you are a human being. (Hi! Nice to meet you, I'm a human being, too.) As such, you are also an emotional being, and so your decisions—like mine and most everyone else's—are more *rationalized* than *rational*. You may not buy this. That's because, through a trick of human nature, we are generally blind to the impact of our own emotions. We see others as emotional, ourselves as level-headed and logical. This isn't just you. It's me, too, and everyone else born to human parents. We like to think we're Spock-like in our ability to think logically when we're anything but. Our tendency to over-estimate our own abilities relative to other people's is so prevalent that psychologists call it the fundamental attribution error. Emphasis on "fundamental." And "attribution." And "error."

Correcting for this quirk of human nature is a lot like correcting for the current when sailing, and just as important. When sailing across a river, for instance, you would point your boat a little ways upstream to counteract the push of the current. If you didn't—that is, if you simply aimed straight at where you want to land—you'd make landfall downstream of your intended destination.

Similar to how you account for the current, you need to account for your emotional state. You need to make adjustments to the way you see the world, because things aren't quite the way you see them. Your emotions provide color that, like a current, pushes you off course.

Also like a current, your emotions affect your trajectory whether you choose to see them or not.

Accept—and Account for—Emotions

If we don't accept and account for our human (read: emotional) tendencies, we can't properly aim for where we want to go. Instead, we develop skills, establish goals, and design processes that all seem to point right at our goals but actually lead us to a point downstream from where we want to go. Then we get there, and we say, "I never should've listened to . . ." or "If only I'd had more money . . ." or "Hey, it's close enough . . ."

What's it called when we do stuff like that? Wait! Don't tell me! I'll remember it. It's on the tip of my tongue.

We can insist that we know what we are doing and that those around us are holding us back. We can tell ourselves we're being reasonable and it's the people around us who are being overly emotional. We can convince ourselves that others are more moronic than ourselves and it's our lot in life to suffer fools. But feelings like these are not at all helpful. They don't get us to our goal. Believing our problems lie in the people around us is tantamount to blaming the current for pushing you off course. *Of course* the current pushed you—but it didn't push you off course! It simply pushed. You missed your target because you chose not to account for it. You chose to fail and—yes, I remember the word!—now you *rationalize* your failure by blaming outside forces.

Sorry, sweetheart, but failure, to one degree or another, becomes all but guaranteed when you ignore the fact that you, too, are prone to make the fundamental attribution error.

I'm not talking about your coworker, your boss, your subordinate, your cube neighbor, your next-door neighbor, your significant other, your family's black sheep, or your friends. I'm talking about YOU. Your boss's subordinate. Your subordinate's boss. Your coworker's coworker. (You get the idea.) It's YOU, buddy.

Before anything else, we—you!—must overcome our flawed humanity by resetting our perspectives and controlling for the emotional current that is always affecting us, whether we are attuned to it or not. And we can do that by closing ourselves off from bad influences and opening ourselves up to the help we will need. Assuming we can tell which is which.

For those of you who don't dig on my sailing analogy, here's a golf story that makes the same point. Please. You must, must, *must* get this concept before we go on.

"All the greens break toward the water," the starter had cautioned me.

I was in Hawaii, playing golf on an oceanside course—because I've been lucky like that—looking out from the tee box to a fairway that I was fairly certain crept uphill as it curved toward the surf. I hit a driver and watched the ball roll toward the ocean . . . and seemingly, impossibly, uphill.

I couldn't believe what I was seeing. Worse, when I got up to the green, I became even more certain that the green ran uphill toward the water . . . the opposite of what the starter had told me. Had he lied? How could my perception be so far off? I needed to putt directly toward the water: should I tap it and let it roll, or should I put some muscle behind it? I was twenty-five feet away, and my decision would have a big impact on what happened next. It was my first time playing this course—my first time playing any course in Hawaii, actually— and I decided to trust my gut.

Big mistake.

With horror, I watched my ball scream past the cup and roll . . . and roll . . . right off the edge of the green and into the pounding surf thirty feet below. It wasn't until the next tee box, when I looked back, that I could see the problem: what had seemed to be an uphill slope was, in reality, an optical illusion caused by an angle in the rock strata. Because I trusted my eyes over the starter's wisdom, my putt never had a chance.

In this analogy, if you haven't figured it out yet, the tilt of the mountain plays the role of my emotions: it was always there, even when I couldn't see it correctly. Ignoring the starter's advice didn't make it go away. All it did was make me less able to sink a putt. My ability to reason was unaffected—I was perfectly capable of processing the information I saw to come to a decision about what to do—but my ability to come up with the correct decision and course of action was obliterated because my rational mind was being fed a bunch of horse caca. Had the next hole not afforded me the view it did, I might have played the rest of the course and rationalized my score based on humidity in the air, competition-cut greens, a hot putter, or who knows what . . . though no matter how firmly I clung to that rationalization, the underlying truth would not have been altered.

OK, do you get it now? How the human condition makes us less able to achieve success and simultaneously blinds us to the problem? How if a person doesn't factor in emotions when using those awesome reasoning skills we humans have, the result is rationalization and not reason? And how blaming the environment and other people doesn't actually change the underlying truth?

Hang onto that awareness—it's the most important takeaway in the book and a recurring theme.

Overcoming Rationalizations

Rationalizations are what we create when we apply reason to a misinterpreted reality. This book is about helping you see reality better.

When you fully commit to your goals, learn the skills necessary to achieve them, and then take full responsibility for breaking down the boulders standing between you and your goals, you ensure fulfillment. If you adopt an attitude that any issue can be overcome and then execute your plans with a vengeance, you ensure success.

This book includes a series of tools, organized into two primary clusters, that are unlike ones you are likely to encounter elsewhere. These tools are designed to take you out of an analytical mind-set and help you get in control of emotional and personality-based success factors that many professionals and managers often fail to consider.

Some of the things in here will seem pretty simple at first blush, until you try to put them into practice. Then you'll see just how challenging it can be to master the emotional side of the equation.

Two Models for Success

There are two models presented in this book that will help you succeed. In a way, these models represent the basics. They are the core, foundational elements to a successful career, applicable across industries, fields, and job titles. At the same time, they are also more advanced than many other models because they focus on aspects of work that many people tend to overlook.

The first is the Magic Moments model, which will help you create an adaptive vision of the future. In short, Magic Moments are moments of deep, personal satisfaction. They are created through a recipe that includes commitment to a proper goal, personal responsibility for creating an environment conducive to success, and a winner's mind-set. Proper goals are realistic; are so tough that achieving them requires you to perform at the edge of your abilities; and provide consistent, actionable feedback on progress. Environments that are conducive to success provide access to the people, places, and resources needed to meet your commitments. And the winner's mind-set is marked by focused determination, persistence, and patience.

The second model presented in the book is the Three Perspectives model. This is an enabling model that will help you engage others to assist you in creating Magic Moments in a complex, networked world. The three perspectives in the model are functional, social, and political. The functional perspective is primarily concerned with what gets done, and functional solutions tend to include working more / better / faster / smarter / harder. This is the default perspective in a work environment. The social perspective is primarily concerned with how work gets done, and social solutions tend to include a handshake. The political perspective is the most conceptual of the three and is unlike the other two perspectives in that it is concerned with the stage on which work gets done, and therefore trumps the other two in importance. At any given moment, you view the world— and are viewed by the world—through these three lenses. To be successful in creating Magic Moments in a corporate environment, it is important to understand how you will be interpreted according to each perspective in order to know how to approach situations for maximum effectiveness.

Remember Everything You've Ever Been Told

Going through this book, you will notice (if you haven't already) that I draw upon stories, metaphors, and examples that are rather mundane in nature. I refer to baseball, school, sailing, golf, and other activities that people can relate to. I do this to get you thinking more creatively about how to address business challenges. The key to success doesn't start with "forget everything you've ever learned about management," nor does it require an inspirational, larger-than-life survival story to be unlocked, either. Everything you need, you already have. The key is to remember to use it, regardless of how you learned it.

| WHAT YOU LEARNED |

- ▶ **Why do so many people struggle to define career success?** *People's mental models for what it takes to excel in their careers have been skewed and don't match reality closely enough to be helpful. TV shows, movies, news programs, and twenty or so years of schooling each, for various reasons, show the working world not quite as it is. As a result, people are practiced at the wrong perspectives and hold expectations that are not quite viable.*

- ▶ **What is the most important factor in determining your success?** *The human element. This comes first, before goals, plans, resources, or anything else.*

- ▶ **What is it called when we blame external factors for problems rather than acknowledge our own failure to correct for emotional currents?** *Rationalizing.*

- ▶ **How will *Super Staying Power* help you?** *It will provide you with a model of success that aligns with the real world by accounting for the emotional realities of life, help you cultivate the proper perspective and skills for implementing that model, and show you how to put it all together into action.*

PART 1

Seeing Success
in a Magic Moment

| IN THIS SECTION |

▶ **What is the relationship between commitment and goal setting?**

▶ **Why is personal responsibility more important than skill development?**

▶ **What drives commitment and personal responsibility?**

Define Success

What does success mean to you? Where are you going? Why do you have this job? What do you hope to achieve in sales / engineering / project management / biotech research / teaching / consulting /whatever? What are your goals? Basic questions. Can you answer them? Without using a cliché?

Ha! Trick questions. Kind of.

Describing success by talking about goals is like describing music by talking about rhythm—it's only part of the concept. In addition to goals, success requires commitment, a conducive environment, a sense of personal responsibility, and the right attitude or mind-set. You could hold just about any job, and if you can create the right conditions, you'll succeed. You may not initially have the house you thought you wanted, or the membership to the club you always pictured yourself having, but you'll experience that feeling of personal satisfaction that allows you to look in the mirror and claim victory over life's challenges. You will know Magic Moments. And because one success tends to beget another, learning to have Magic Moments— on any level—will set you up for a lifetime of future victories. Below is a quick overview of the components of success; in the chapters that follow, I provide a model for understanding how they work together and explore each component in more depth.

Goals and the Power of Commitment

People often take pride in establishing logical, rationally determined goals. But like a boater ignoring the current, failing to recognize and correct for our emotions when establishing goals opens us to the possibility that our actions will leave us downstream of our intended destination. For goals to have power, they must be achievable. And to be achievable, their first prerequisite is to be matched to a high degree of commitment. Commitment provides focused awareness, which in turn allows us to direct our energies. Commitment helps us zero in on our intended destination and helps us attune to everything, including our emotional states, that may be propelling us toward or pushing us away from our destination in any given moment. Without commitment, goals are spots across the river we cannot reach, no better than fantasies or wishes.

When people talk about the power of goals, what they really are talking about is the power of commitment. Goals allow us to pick a direction; commitment gives us the power to achieve them. The goal-setting process, generally considered a process in which the picture of an intended goal is refined, actually serves a second, equally important purpose: it is the process by which commitment is reinforced. Goals alone are nothing; it is when you commit to, work toward, and live for them that they become something.

Personal Responsibility and Your Environment

After commitment to your goal, the next most important element to success is an environment conducive to what you are trying to achieve. And since what you are doing is building toward a vision that exists in your head and not yet in reality, chances are you are going to have to create at least some of that environment yourself. As a training facilitator, I have an interesting perspective on people's willingness to create their own environments. The ones who aren't willing to create the environment they need are quick to externalize their problems; they are the ones raising their hands, saying, "Hey, why am I here? I know this stuff. You know who should be taking this class? You know who really needs to hear this message? Legal / contracts / customer service / marketing / ops / tech / management / corporate / the sales office / purchasing / manufacturing / the warehouse guys / our drivers / dispatch / floor supervisors / processing / HR / finance. . . . Let's get *those guys* in here!" When the idea of personal responsibility clicks in their heads, they stop making comments like this. That's the point when real skill development starts to occur—before that moment, these participants are more likely to approach skill development in an academic, philosophical way rather than a visceral, I-know-exactly-when-and-why-I-need-that-skill sort of way. In other words, "skill development" can be pretty much a waste of time.

When the concept of personal responsibility snaps into place, it feels like a punch to the gut. It triggers a person to look around and say, "OK, I see what's required to achieve my goal—I see what I've committed to—and it's a lot. Let's make sure this is where I want to make my stand." At the same time, fear disappears. Fear of feedback, fear of failure, fear of success—they vanish. The future becomes a function of time and skill and nothing else. It is now possible to consider the environment and determine exactly what is required to achieve the goal, in terms of skills, resources, relationships, and location. We ask ourselves if it is more effective to develop particular skills or recruit teammates who already have them. We consider where we are and whether or not we would have better access to tools by moving someplace else. We refine the milestones and timelines we had set previously. The goal gave us our destination; commitment, the power to achieve it. Our environment provides us leverage. But our environment is incredibly complex, offering a vast array of resources, relationships, and potential advantages. How can we possibly manage all of it, and quickly, too, so that we can put it to use? By applying ourselves—by taking 100 percent personal responsibility for shaping it to our needs.

Commitment and Responsibility Are Products of Attitude

Commitment and responsibility, even when coupled with goals and skills, are still not enough to create success. You also need the right attitude. You have to have a mind-set that is focused, persistent, and open. Have you ever heard someone say to you, "Trust me," and immediately think, *No way?* When you want to convince someone of something, knowing what to say isn't enough—you've got to put the right attitude behind the words to make them believable. Similarly, you'll need to put the right attitude behind your actions. Ultimately, your ability to stay committed to your goals and maintain the leverage afforded by your environment is a function of your attitude.

Goals, environment, and attitude: these are the components of the Magic Moment.

But first, a story.

WHAT YOU LEARNED

▶ **What is the relationship between commitment and goal setting?** *If goal setting is picking a spot across a river you want to reach, commitment is correcting for the current. Without commitment, you will consistently land downstream of your goal.*

▶ **Why is personal responsibility more important than skill development?** *Without a sense of personal responsibility, skill development is an academic exercise. Skill development has much more impact if it occurs after you have taken responsibility for shaping your environment and making it conducive to your success.*

▶ **What drives commitment and personal responsibility?** *It's attitude, sweet pea.*

Magic Moments

My Perfect Day

The call came in at eight P.M. It was Todd, my ski instructor, inviting me to ski with him and his friends the following day. This was a pretty special call. To understand why, it is helpful to have some background about Todd.

Todd has been a ski instructor his entire adult life. He currently instructs instructors, and it is no wonder why: as a teacher, he has that uncanny ability to simultaneously knock you off your pedestal and build you up at the same time. He shows you how to be great, but he also scrubs you clean of every last whiff of arrogance. Todd has been my instructor for about fourteen years. His wife, also an instructor, has been my wife's ski teacher for nearly thirty years. Our families are friends. But the importance of this phone call goes beyond my

25

respect for Todd as an instructor or our personal relationship. It has to do with who Todd is as a person.

One memorable evening years ago, Todd invited me to have dinner at his house, which at the time was brand-new. The first thing I noticed when I walked in was a beautiful staircase, made of rough-hewn, half moon–shaped logs (flat side on top, for stepping). I commented on it. Todd's immediate response was to laugh, "I thought chopping that tree down was tough! Let me tell you the story about how I got it into the house!"

My chin hit the floor—but wait, it gets better. Todd did more than design and build the staircase. He also dug the foundation, a good portion of it with a shovel. Apparently, someone was late delivering the backhoe, and Todd didn't feel like waiting idly by for his house to come together when he could be putting it together himself. (Talk about a get-it-done attitude: commitment to the project, personal responsibility for the environment, focus, persistence, openness, initiative . . . it was all there. Todd's experience building his house was, for him, as special as my perfect ski day, with one difference: my Magic Moment ski day is a memory, whereas his Magic Moment is now the home he sleeps in every night.)

On my tour of his new castle, I noticed a small skull, a hunting trophy, at the top of the staircase. A mountain cat skull. With a hole in the forehead. And next to the skull? The arrow that made the hole.

Now I don't know about you, but I don't think I'd ever like to be in a position to have to make that shot. I reckon if I'm putting an arrow through the forehead of a mountain lion, two things are true: one, I'm not the only one hunting that day, and two, that cat is in pouncing range when I shoot it. When I asked Todd about that, he was nonplussed. He even changed the subject. "Oh, that? Yeah, it was pretty serious. But I wasn't half as scared as I was when I had a moose chasing me in circles around a tree for three hours . . . or—did I ever tell you about when we had a bear up in the tree out front?"

(For years after this evening, I felt, on a certain level, like my man card was not the same card he carried. I started filleting my own fish at restaurants. It wasn't much, but I had to do something, you know?)

Todd's larger-than-life persona applied to his skiing as well. Whenever I took a lesson with a different instructor, if I told him who my regular instructor was, the typical response I got was similar to what I imagine would happen if a guitar student at the local music shop mentioned that he often jammed with his neighbor, Eddie Van Halen. Even back in the day, I learned that many of the instructors took lessons with Todd. Most of them seemed just as impressed by him as I was. Others were petrified of the man.

So this invitation to come skiing with Todd and his friends, as a peer rather than a student, signaled that I had arrived. The invitation meant a lot to me. Todd, who built his house with his bare hands and taught instructors how to ski and could basically do anything better than anyone, was saying, "Hey, Jase, c'mon, you're one of us." It was important validation, which I'd guess anyone who has worked to master a skill—big or small—will understand.

Indeed, I distinctly remember being on the phone when he asked me to join the group. Quite suddenly, the clouds parted, the sun shone down directly on me, and cherubs began playing lovely music on their harps. It was euphoric. It was also a bit strange, as it was eight o'clock at night and dark and I was inside my apartment, but it was a spectacular scene nonetheless.

I awoke the next day to perfect conditions: eight inches of fresh snow, blue skies, forty-degree weather. A T-shirt day! It was truly as if the heavens had smiled upon me. I got myself ready and made my way to the base, where I met my new friends. I was one of two people, out of nine, not wearing ski patrol or ski instructor jackets . . . and the other one was decked head to toe in Solomon gear. He was a manufacturer's rep. I was clearly out of my league.

With this group, normal mountain rules did not apply. In bounds, out of bounds, no bounds. We skied at the resort, we skied the backcountry, we skied . . . whatever the other guys felt like skiing. Our unofficial motto seemed to be "Have slope, will ski. Fast."

If you've never spent time in the mountains, it can be difficult to imagine how much a part of the world you feel when you're out there and things are going well. Skiing virgin powder that hadn't been touched all season—thigh-high stuff that throws spray up over your shoulders once you break through its thin, crispy coating—you are blind to everything and out of earshot of the world. You are this tiny thing hurtling down a slope, yet very much connected and squarely at the center of your own universe.

It was some pretty serious skiing, with pretty serious consequences for anyone who made a mistake. No one needed to tell us about the dangers of hitting a tree; every one of us skiing that day had lost a friend to a tree-related skiing accident. In the backcountry, a simple fall could prove disastrous. If a ski popped off out here, it could disappear forever, and we were a long hike from home. However, thinking about such things is a sure way to manifest them, so I tucked these concerns into the recesses of my mind and ignored them as we cut fresh tracks, ducked between pines, flew through bumps, and raced down the corduroy faster than city dwellers drive most of the time. I fell, often, but when I needed to be perfect, I was perfect.

Sometimes I could keep up with the rest of the group. Other times, like when I was navigating pine trees and trying to avoid the quicksand-like powder beneath the branches, I couldn't. I alternated between getting down the mountain in record time and thinking about . . . getting . . . around . . . this next . . . rock . . . aaaand . . . holy . . . crap-not-much-space-between-those-trees-turn-NOW-moving-fast-whoa-where'd-this-dip-come-from-I'm-gonna-get-catapulted-here-we-go-*wheeeeee!*-I'm-flying!-now-where-the-#$%!-am-I-supposed-to-*land*?!

Silence.

Breathe.

Look around, find friends.

Smile. Bend a bit because legs are shaking from the exertion.

Relax for a moment until someone asks, "Hey, who wants to do that one again?!"

In the late afternoon sun, as I sat outside with my beer and thought about what had happened out there that day, I thanked the mountain for testing me without breaking me. I had a flash of all the runs I had done that day—every turn, every wipeout, every kicker—and I thought to myself, "This is perfect. It truly doesn't get any better than this."

Your Perfect Day

Inevitably, when I tell this story to a group, people's minds wander away from my ski day to events from their own lives when they experienced that same feeling—that same sense of *perfection*. Maybe it was during a special event, or perhaps it was on some unremarkable Thursday when you managed to hit all green lights and everything just went your way for a change. Whatever it was, you've had one. At least one. Your perfect day. Can you recall it? Do you remember that feeling?

That was your Magic Moment, your moment of deep, personal contentment, brought about by the perfection of the moment. That was your taste of success.

The Explanation

Ever have someone explain the punch line of a joke you told? I have. It stinks. It's even worse when it's not a joke but the mechanics of your all-time favorite experience being explained to you.

Shortly after my magical ski day, I went back to work, which at the time meant going back to an office where I was the lone M.B.A. swimming in a sea of Ph.Ds. Naturally I was asked about the trip, and so I shared my experience, in colorful and somewhat poetic terms.

Not that I have anything against Ph.D.s—quite the contrary, I married one—but on this particular day, the particular doctor of philosophy with whom I was speaking was particularly academic-ish. She looked at me and nodded as I spoke. She continued to nod long after I had finished my story. (Don't be fooled: nodding is a meaningless, practiced behavior meant to keep others talking. Shrinks are masters of it. They call it "acknowledging" behavior. I call it a great way to feign interest in others when you don't care to engage.) Eventually, when she realized I wasn't going to give her any more material, she stood up and announced, "Well, sounds like you had a great time!"

I parried, glad to have moved from soliloquy to conversation: "I sure did! Have you ever been—"

She cut me off. "Let me explain why you had so much fun."

What?! Explain? That's not how a conversation is supposed to work!

It was too late. She was on a mission. Before I knew it, she stood at the white board in my office, marker in hand. She proceeded to explain how my experience could be described as a moment of deep, personal contentment. How the wiring in my brain colluded with various environmental factors to produce the special feeling of that day. How the structure of the day's events had enabled me to sustain that feeling. She mentioned how her model was supported by recent research by Mihaly Csikszentmihalyi. That was about all the explaining I could take. I threw her out of my office before she could get much more else out, but by then, it was too late. My Magic Moment, like the punch line of a favorite joke, was in shambles. I had had enough.

The Discovery

I stewed, off and on, for a long while. Eventually, though, I decided I was done being angry. The memory was too important, too much a part of me, to allow it to be tarnished by a single conversation. I needed to find a way to get the romance back.

Much to my surprise, it was easy.

When I actually stopped and thought about it, I could find no bullet holes: the memory was still complete, still perfect. Despite having been broken down and parsed, I could still relive it and recapture the feelings from that day. The romance of the moment was still alive and well.

I stood there, thinking about my skiing experience, and as I did so, I was transported right back to the first phone call. Right there, on a sidewalk in downtown Chicago, the clouds parted once again, trumpets played, and cherubs came down from the sky to play their harps just for me.

You should have seen the faces on the people around me.

The memory was as intensely satisfying as the original event had been. And that's when I discovered the real magic: these moments permeate your soul and become a part of you. They fill every fiber of your being and can't be undone by the ramblings of some pompous windbag.

True success is much more than a moment in time. It is a moment in the more transcendental sense of the word. Success stops time. It expands you into something more. It obliterates fear and connects you to something bigger than yourself. Success is not necessarily happiness, but to hear people describe it, you can tell where happiness fits into the equation.

Success—via Magic Moments—happens when you rise above the human condition and become something more.

I felt like I had just discovered a perfect joke that could be explained and would be just as funny afterward as it had been before.

After the discovery, what went through my head next was a flurry of activity that went something like this:

- ▶ I just wasted time being angry. Oops.
- ▶ I hope I haven't said anything that I'll regret. I may owe someone an apology. Do I owe someone an apology?
- ▶ If I know the elements of how to create this deep contentment, and understanding them doesn't preclude me from enjoying them in the moment, then I can do more than explain them—I can create them!

▶ If I could get this feeling of contentment in my personal life, why couldn't I experience it at work, too? No rule says I can't . . . right?

▶ Even if there were a rule, that's precisely the kind of rule I'd enjoy breaking.

▶ Success in life just got easy. I can overlay this idea atop any area of my life!

▶ I'm going to have to take full ownership of my problems. That may be tough, as I don't have sufficient authority to control my world directly. I'm going to have to figure something out.

That last point in particular scared me a bit: there were definitely things standing between me and deep, personal contentment, and those things definitely seemed external in nature. Alright, I need to be honest. There were *people* standing between me and deep personal contentment: people holding me back, clipping my wings, stealing my thunder, telling me no, controlling my client interaction, dictating my billing. But, according to this model, none of what they did mattered. The model looked wrong but felt right. Really right—cherubs and harps kind of right. I took a deep breath.

I was on another tee box, being told the slope of the course, and again my eyes were telling me something else. If I was going to use the model, I was going to have to trust what I knew instead of what I saw. I was going to have to trust that I could own my own destiny, even though it appeared that I didn't seem to have sufficient power to do so.

My brain raced, trying to remember what my colleague had said the components of a Magic Moment were. Oh, no, I had kicked her out of my office too soon! I needed her back.

She had some 'splainin' to do.

I went back to the office, found my new favorite Ph.D. (other than my wife), and asked for a more detailed explanation of what had happened to me on the slopes. This time, I was the one using a writing utensil. I didn't want to miss a thing.

What follows is what I learned that day.

The Magic Moment

A Magic Moment is a moment of deep, personal contentment that is the result of an intensely satisfying experience. Magic Moments are those moments when you completely lose yourself, when consciousness moves at unconscious speeds, and that stay with you forever. You close your eyes and you're back there: the sights, the smells, the sounds; everything is preserved.

Magic Moments are caused by an understandable, predictable, manageable set of conditions. You can learn to create the conditions necessary to foster Magic Moments, and when you do, you can string multiple Moments together, or include other people, allowing you to create Magic Moments on a large scale. No, your life probably won't become one long, extended Magic Moment. (It could, though, if all the elements of your personal equation came together just right—and how cool would that be? You could change your name to Buddha.) Ups and downs are to be expected. The key is to focus on turning the ups into Magic Moments. And because they are actionable, adaptive, and universal, Magic Moments can be used to provide the foundation for career success in any job, in any field, in any industry.

Creating Contentment

You probably already are pretty good at creating Magic Moments in your personal life. Likely, you create them frequently. This entire book would probably be superfluous if the subject weren't work but how to hang out with friends or how to enjoy a hobby. Not that we're always successful in areas outside of work, but the idea of living in the moment to make the relationship / activity / event a Magic Moment seems to come more naturally to people when discussing non-work activities.

Still, there's no rule that states that we *can't* have Magic Moments at work. So if you are going to be at work for thirty, forty, fifty hours a week, why not try? We often put barriers between ourselves and work-related Magic Moments. Why? Opening ourselves up to Magic Moments at work can help us establish the framework for our career success story, and Heaven knows we could use some more success stories. Let's open ourselves up and go create some.

Opening Yourself Up to a Magic Moment

So how do you open yourself up to a Magic Moment? You need a whopping total of three things: you need a goal you can commit to, an environment you can shape, and a winner's attitude that is focused, persistent, and open.

That's it; when these three elements are in place, voilà, Magic Moment.

Ready to dive in?

Awesome. Let's do this.

WHAT YOU LEARNED

▶ **What are Magic Moments, and why are they important?** *Magic Moments are moments of deep, personal contentment that are caused by an intensely satisfying experience. Magic Moments are important because they provide actionable, adaptive, and universal models for success that can be applied to any job, in any field, in any industry.*

▶ **What are the three main elements of a Magic Moment?** *To experience a Magic Moment, you need a goal that you can commit to, an environment you can shape that is conducive to your success, and a winner's attitude that is focused, persistent, and open.*

A Goal You Can Commit To

Understanding Goals

I have fielded a number of questions about goals from people over the years. I've also asked a number of questions about goals over the years. Questions such as:

▶ Why are some ridiculously ambitious goals inspiring, while others are simply ridiculous?

▶ Why do people sometimes warn that "easy" goals don't stick, while other times they say having "easier" goals is responsible? (Low-hanging fruit, they call it.)

▶ What happens when I'm not in control of my goals, like when a boss assigns one to me?

▶ Should I have multiple goals? What if they conflict?

Lots of books, consultants, and experts have explored the concept of goals, intellectually defining them based on behaviors and outcomes. We have SMART goals, stretch goals, operating goals, financial goals, balanced goals, strategic goals, tactical goals, and life goals, to name a few. And yet, despite all the attention given to the topic, our goals have led us to an economic train wreck, massive levels of debt, depleted natural resources, and highly stressful living.

How can it be that trying to do the right thing led to such backward results? Let's find out. Following are ten common mistakes inherent in the way most people approach goal setting, regardless of which type of goal they are creating.

Mistake #1: Over-Relying on Visualization

"If I just think about my goal all the time, it will come true."

Hi. Nice to meet you. I'm sorry, what did you say your name was? Cinderella?

Thinking is not a strategy for goal attainment. In fact, as it doesn't seem to be required much even in school these days, thinking isn't really a strategy for much of anything anymore. Which is too bad.

When people talk about "intention manifestation" and "becoming a vibrational match with your goal," they're talking about engaging that reptilian back part of your brain known as your subconscious. When that part of your mind is engaged and focused, you can think / worry / doubt / plan / do whatever you want in the front of your mind and it won't matter. That back part is where the power is. But merely thinking about something isn't enough to engage that back part. We need thoughts to be emotionally charged. If Napoleon Hill got anything wrong, it was the title of his book, *Think and Grow Rich*. It should have been more like, *Meld Emotional Commitment with Thinking and Grow Rich*.

Mistake #2: Constantly Refining as You Go

"I'll put a stake in the ground and refine my goal as I go."

Aaaand . . . let me know when you've put enough little holes in the ground—we can play connect the dots.

Every time you refine your goal, even just a little, you change your focus and the whole process of engaging that back part of your mind starts over. Yes, it's true that you will have to change your goal as you learn more—goal setting is a process, not an event. And yes, I'm going to spend a fair amount of time outlining the feedback process through which those changes are made. But those changes need to be deliberate and careful.

Constantly refining a goal without intentional planning leads to you taking a lot of tactical steps that don't lead anywhere.

Mistake #3: Starting Too Small

"I'll start with some easy, small goals and work my way up."

A friend of mine from junior high thought this way. I remember him asking me in middle school why I worked so hard and telling me he worked just hard enough to get by. We were twelve. He said that when he got to high school and grades started to matter more, he'd work harder. Would you be surprised to learn his plan never materialized? He was a good guy. Nice guy. I liked him. But I remember that conversation, and I know he had potential he never realized. He started too small. He never challenged himself, he got bored, and he tuned out from his own life.

Those who advocate taking this path tend to argue that the momentum gained through small, early wins can provide the foundation for bigger, future wins. That's not entirely true. Small wins work when there is a big, specific goal already committed to and what you need is early momentum. Like in the story of the boy who went away for a year to learn karate from a wise master.

You haven't heard it?

The short version goes like this: the sensei had the boy come live with him for a year at his oceanside home to study. The sensei told the boy formal classes would begin when the boy was ready, and in the meantime the boy was to help fill a giant fish pond in the garden with water from the ocean. The sensei demanded that the boy walk several hundred yards into the sea in order to get "clean" water. A year went by and the boy returned to visit his family, never having taken any classes. They asked how the training was coming, and the boy cried out in shame, "I haven't learned a thing! All I've done is go into the sea and collect water for his stupid pond!" With that he slammed his foot down on the oak floor, breaking one of the support logs in two.

"But Jase," you say, "that's a perfect example of why it pays to stay focused on small goals—every day, do a little something, and in time, you achieve your goal!"

True, but only because the boy spent every minute of his days focused on his one and only big goal of learning karate. No one needed to instruct him to focus on strengthening his legs, gaining endurance, and learning balance as he walked through hundreds of yards of surf every day. Because he was so committed to his goal, his body did those things automatically, subconsciously. That's what made his daily treks so effective. Goal, big. Progression, small.

Without his commitment to that larger goal, however, he would have gotten far less value from his walks through the waves. And that's the problem with this approach: it presupposes a commitment to a larger goal, without warning the people who are like my middle school friend that without a prior commitment, all it does is train you to aim low.

Set your big goal first, and then establish interim goals that help you get there.

Mistake #4: Setting Goals That Sound Specific but Aren't

"I want to make a million dollars by the time I'm twenty-five."

That sounds great, doesn't it? Nice and specific: you've got an amount, you've got a timeframe. Right? Wrong.

Are you talking about earnings or savings? Cumulative earnings or annual earnings? Are you implying you'll make this money while living a lavish lifestyle, or are you allowing yourself to get there as a miser? Although it sounds specific, this goal falls apart under closer scrutiny.

Here's a better idea: figure out what you want to do with that money and make it your goal to do *that* by the time you're twenty-five. Like "I want to own my own house" or "I want to support my parents." The money you need to accomplish those goals will come as a matter of course.

Mistake #5: Being Swayed by the Opinions of Others

"Everyone's gonna love this."

Humans tend to change their goals based on the opinions of others, even when they don't mean to. As a species, we can be *so* weak-minded.

Yeah, I mean you and me, too.

Back in the 1950s, a fellow by the name of Solomon Asch did a series of psychological experiments with people like you and me to show just how weak-minded we can be.

He had people look at a picture of two lines, one of which was noticeably longer than the other, and declare which was longer. Not surprisingly, nearly 100 percent of all participants with a brain got this question right. But then he did something interesting. He put those people like you and me at a table with other people and then asked everyone to declare, publicly, which line was longer. And you know what he found? He found that the people who declared last would frequently say whatever all the people before them had said.

Now this may not seem like much, because if one line was obviously so much longer than the other that no one got it wrong, then of course the last person would agree with his or her peers. Where's the "big whoop" in that?

Well, here's the big whoop: all the other people at the table were confederates. Plants. Actors. They were all in on the experiment. And they were up to no good. Their instructions told them to lie and say that the shorter line looked longer. Or vice versa. The last person to speak was the only person not in on the joke. Er, experiment.

The confederates gave an obviously wrong answer. All of them. The first person would flat out *lie*, and then the next person in the group would agree with the wrong answer. On and on it went, until it was the last person's turn to speak, at which point the social pressure to conform had been built up quite a bit.

So much so, in fact, that the final person often gave a knowingly false answer so as not to buck the will of the group. Moreover, when called out on the mistake, that person tended to blame his or her own poor eyesight. He or she seemed unaware of (or unwilling to admit to) the impact of social pressure!

After enough people had behaved this way, Asch jumped up on the table and shouted, "Eureka!"

Or something like that.

Asch's findings weren't with weird people. They were with folks like you and me. Social pressure, as it turns out, is a powerful force.

So powerful, in fact, that we probably need to throw out the goals you've set for yourself because, like the people in Asch's experiments, your goals have likely been unduly influenced by your interactions with others, and you probably don't even know it. If you sat and negotiated with a boss, spouse, or someone else for your goals, if you lowered your goals because a teacher once told you to aim low, or if you set your goals based on the idea that the world is all doom and gloom (because that's what you see on TV), then we need to treat your goals as suspect. If what you love about your goals is the response they'll get from others, then you *definitely* need to treat your goals as suspect.

Here's a quick test you can use to see if you're the type of person who might sometimes fall prey to social conditioning:

1. Are you alive? If yes, you probably fall prey to social conditioning, at least sometimes.

There is no question #2.

And here's a quick example of how insidious social pressure can be: have you ever set a diet goal for yourself? Lose ten pounds, bulk up until you can bench press 450, something like that?

Quick—what was your dieting goal? Go grab a pen and write it down. Use the margin of this book if you need to, but write it down. Declare!

OK, now get ready, because there is actually a correct answer in this case. (I know, in today's day and age, it's very en vogue to do quizzes with "no single right answer." Sometimes it's necessary for there to be wrong answers.) The correct answer in this case is: *My goal is to live a lifestyle that makes dieting unnecessary.* Moreover, you *know* that is the right answer.

Did you say that? Or something like it?

If you didn't, don't worry, you're in good company—most people I ask this question of don't get it.

Think about your response. Did you limit it based on the way I framed the question? Did you try to answer the specific question I asked? Are you so accustomed to talking about five- and ten-pound diets that that's what came out? Whatever the reason, if you didn't provide the right answer, you've just felt the powerful, subtle impact of social conformity. (Maybe with a little authority pressure added in, too, à la Stanley Milgram.) This is worth keeping in mind not just when setting your professional goals, but in life generally.

Mistake #6: Glossing Over the Details

"Looks great, let's do it. . . . We can figure out the details later."

Ever been disappointed by the reality of a vacation spot that seemed enchantingly perfect online? Or by a person whose résumé (or photo) led you to have higher hopes than reality could support?

A goal can work the same way. It can feel good from afar, yet when you dive into it, it sometimes reveals itself as untenable. If you don't know the details, you don't yet know the goal. Best to treat goal setting as a process rather than a discrete event, so as to give yourself time to get intimate with your goals at a detailed level!

Mistake #7: Being Too Rigid

"I can picture the world I want."

Got a mental picture of success? That's seriously great . . . until your world changes and renders your vision obsolete. To wit:

You set your sights on a new car—a BMW!—and tell all your friends that's what you intend to buy because BMWs are the best. Then BMW changes the body style and you hate, hate, hate the new model. *Now what?* Buy an Audi and explain to your friends that you were wrong about which car was best? Or suck it up and buy a car you don't like?

You decide you want to become CEO of your company, but then a scandal sends the whole place into bankruptcy two months before you are scheduled to take the helm. *Now what?*

You picture yourself playing catch with your future son, taking him to ball games, teaching him to wrestle, going fishing . . . and then you have daughters. *Now what?*

Etc., etc., etc.

One thing changes in your environment, and your whole picture of success changes. As much as you are in control of yourself, you also live in a big, big world where sometimes all you can do is react. You need to be committed, yet flexible.

Mistake #8: Over-Relying on Analytical Models

"Hey, I hope you're not talking about SMART goals, because I like my SMART goals!"

Of course you do. We all do. People have this general tendency to eschew ambiguity and embrace things that are organized, analytical, clean, and orderly. And that's what SMART goals provide: a world that's specific, measurable, attainable, realistic, timely. That's great stuff. For a checklist. Too bad real life is more than a checklist.

On their own, SMART goals are necessary but insufficient. SMART goals help establish the transactional elements of what needs to be done, but they leave something big totally unaccounted for. Here's something you can do to experience what I'm talking about: pick up a book on painting. Follow the instructions. Create SMART goals for yourself that have you painting and practicing new techniques every day. Now ask yourself, "How many years will it take me to become a master?"

I'm sorry, what was that? You'll likely *never* become a master? Why do you say that . . . aren't you using SMART goals?!

Clearly, art is more than those technical aspects of the craft that can be captured with SMART goals. Now here's a surprise: ditto career management . . . and leadership, marriage, athletics, team building, math, and life.

Mistake #9: Obsessing over Balance

Yes, balance! Let's chop our lives into so many little boxes and create little goals for each box:

- ☐ Spouse? *Check.*
- ☐ House? *Check.*
- ☐ Job? *Check.*
- ☐ Better job? *Check.*
- ☐ Luxury car? *Check.*
- ☐ Church on Sunday? (Oh, you're Jewish? Synagogue on Friday night?) *Check.*
- ☐ 2.4 kids? *Check.*
- ☐ Mental well-being reestablished via biannual trip to remote beach paradise? *Check.*

On second thought, no.

Chasing balance has wrecked the institution of marriage, gutted our neighborhoods, turned work into an unfulfilling grind for too many, eroded our core values, withered spirituality into empty ritual, and institutionalized arrogance. . . . I'll end there—it gets really depressing after that. And still, no balance. Suffice to say, if you haven't already guessed, I'm not buying the balance rap.

Balance, as a goal unto itself, makes no sense. Nobody says, "Follow your balance." Nobody inspires us to "Follow your passions from eight to five, and then turn them off." Yet that's pretty much what we try to do with our scorecards and goals—put our passions into so many little boxes and balance them all. We may want to be in balance, but our goal is not the balance itself but the ability to engage in those various activities that we are holding in balance!

Balance is a natural, long-term outcome of following your passions, not a goal. Treating balance as a goal actually can be quite dangerous. To get good at something is to dare to allow that thing to consume you. When you lead with the clock, you prohibit that from ever being the case in any area of your life and become destined for mediocrity.

I awoke with the idea for my first book, *How to Self-Destruct*, in my head at three A.M. What if I had just gone back to bed? How many brilliant ideas, wonderful movies, great books, and savvy business ideas never see the light of day every year because the person who has them simply goes back to sleep, literally or figuratively? How many ideas are lost because—sorry!—it's time to catch the train, eat breakfast, wake up, go to bed, go to class, hit the gym . . . ? If you don't yet live your passions, chasing balance will ensure that you never do.

Mistake #10: Overemphasizing Business "Goals"

"What about financial and operational goals, don't we have to have those?"

Yes, and let's be careful, because semantics matter. Expected financial and operational results are necessary for planning purposes—this is true. But just because a number is forward-looking doesn't make it a worthy goal. We can call them "goals" all we want, but not all goals are created equal. These particular goals are really more forecasting and management tools than actual goals. Who commits to 9.43 percent growth in sales? Somebody does, sure, but generally, people commit to things like *building great companies*, *keeping their jobs*, or *outperforming their peers*. Financial targets are how they meet those commitments.

Pretending that people will readily commit themselves to business "goals" is lazy management and one of the great obstacles holding organizations back. Douglas McGregor said it in *The Human Side of Enterprise*, Jim Collins said it in *Good to Great*, and I'm saying it again: organizational objectives work when they align with employees' desire to be part of something bigger. Give me the business objective, just also tell me why that objective is important. Give me the goal *behind* the goal.

Now, I know many people respond well to clean, focused goals. I get that. And if financially and operationally oriented SMART goals help you and your team focus, then by all means keep using them. But be aware that when you have success, it's not because of the goals but people's commitment to the security and structure those goals bring.

Don't freak out if you see yourself in some of the preceding traps. Even great goals will have elements from one or more of these traps. But to avoid these traps and set yourself up to have Magic Moments at work, you're going to want to approach goal setting a bit differently.

Goal Setting: Make an Adaptive Plan

If you tie your passion to a too rigid, rational picture of success, you risk having the whole thing shattered by events outside of your control. For instance: the market tanks; does that mean you suddenly can't be happy? I'm not saying life didn't just get harder, but . . . so what? Who says you can't be happy unless the Dow Jones Industrial Average is above 12,000? Or that you have to retire exactly on the day you expected to retire? I understand, you had plans that must now change, but where is the law that says change has to be a problem? Oh, wait, I found it: the law is called the law of requisite variety, coined by W. Ross Ashby in 1956 in his book *An Introduction to Cybernetics*. The law of requisite variety says, in essence, that if your environment absorbs shocks faster than you do, you're going to get thrown for a loop. So if you want to have a lasting, successful career during times of change, you are going to need a model that allows you to remain flexible and dispassionate as this economic roller coaster cycles through its twists, turns, and drops.

For instance, would you have the presence of mind to take advantage of the need to start over by . . . starting over? Wasn't there something else you wanted to do with your life, given the chance? Well, if the "golden handcuffs" are gone, then what's still keeping you in place? Rigid, rational pictures of success can become traps, especially during turbulent times. When they do, that's bad.

But, so how do we change the pictures in our heads? We don't want a process that constantly requires us to adapt to another new reality—too cumbersome. We want something that's light and adaptive; something that helps us cope with the inevitable, relentless, and extreme variability that has come to mark our lives; something that makes us impervious to change.

How do we ensure that our goals are adaptive, moving us closer to our Magic Moments regardless of what's happening around us?

Real

Goals must be real—they must abide by the immutable laws of nature, such as those that govern physics, electromagnetism, and human dynamics. (Yes, human dynamics follow a set of laws. Yes, the implication here is that you and I are predictable. No, I don't expect you to like that statement. No, I don't expect you'll agree with it, either . . . at least not yet. And no, neither how you feel about it nor what you believe changes the fact that you are, indeed, predictable.)

An example of an impossible goal would be to wire my home to run off a nine-volt battery. My energy consumption rate simply requires more than that little square battery has to offer. It wouldn't happen.

Goals must be real.

Tough

The first question you should have upon reading a header like this is, "How tough?"

Your goal needs to be so tough that if you bring anything less than your best, you will not achieve your goal. And even if you bring your A-game, you *still* may not achieve your goal. If you're not flirting with the line between "damn near impossible" and "impossible," your goal is not tough enough.

Goals don't need to be awe-inspiringly big, only tough enough to force you to concentrate and stay committed. If when you go to bed each night you don't harbor some doubt about your ability to nail it, you're slumming it, living shy of the level of Magic Moments.

Which raises a question: where exactly is the line between nearly impossible and impossible? The answer is: there is no line. Every time you set yourself a goal of doing the impossible and do it, the line moves.

How awesome is that!

(Someone, quick: find me a nine-volt battery and the blueprints for my house!)

Feedbacking

Often the only difference between a real goal and an impossible goal is feedback. Not just any feedback, mind you, but progress feedback.

Something that lets you know you are moving toward or away from your goal. With process feedback, the impossible sometimes becomes doable—even if just barely.

In the world of skiing, feedback is easy: if I'm upright and balanced, I'm doing just fine. If I am in any other position, I've got a problem.

In business, where everyone keeps track of financial metrics, we tend to forget these measures are lagging indicators of performance; we often confuse them with the more actionable, in-the-moment progress feedback we need to be successful.

It's natural to think that if we were successful last time, then we will probably be successful next time, too. In times of stasis, that works great. But in today's world, I just checked my newspaper—which just went bankrupt, by the way—and according to what I'm seeing about the newspaper industry, car industry, and banking industry, not so much stasis these days. What worked before probably won't work anymore moving forward. And by "probably," I mean "definitely." Which, if all I've got is financial data that shows me last year's results, is a problem.

Certainly, we need to be careful not to get caught up in measuring activity and lose sight of results, but when change comes at us as rapidly as it does today—when it's often faster and cheaper to experiment than to plan—we need to make sure we're getting forward-indicating feedback that helps us move ahead of the curve, not behind it.

Constructing meaningful feedback loops that connect leading performance indicators with results will take time, experimentation, and a playful attitude. Easier said than done . . . but doable. One trick: when isolating cause and effect, do so inclusive of relationships, quality of communications, and other interpersonal variables. (I'll talk more about why this information is relevant in the second half of the book. For now, consider this: when a friend opts out of dinner plans, we naturally ask ourselves if it was due to the choice of restaurant . . . or the company. But in analogous situations at work, we tend to assume the decision was related to the restaurant and get angry if anyone insinuates that it may have been the company.) By bringing more inclusive reasoning to your workplace goals, you allow for richer, more actionable feedback loops and take an important step toward giving yourself more staying power and making yourself indispensable.

These are the criteria for appropriately adaptive goals. The size of the goal is irrelevant. It doesn't have to be awe-inspiring. It doesn't have to be big. It doesn't have to be terribly ambitious. Big goals may be necessary to align teams, but at the individual level, a small goal works just as well as a big one . . . as long as it is meaningful and worthy of your commitment, and as long as it is real, tough, and feedbacking.

WHAT YOU LEARNED

▶ **What common problems do people run into when setting goals?** *Intellectually based goals fall prey to common, predictable, and easily rationalized glitches in the human psyche, such as our need to conform to social pressure.*

▶ **What's wrong with focusing on a mental "vision" of your desired state?** *If you tie your passion to a too rigid, rational picture of success, you risk having the whole thing shattered by events outside of your control. You need goals that are adaptive.*

▶ **What are the three elements of a Magic Moment–inducing goal?** *Real, tough, and feedbacking: goals must respect natural laws, including those that govern human behavior. Goals should be so tough that if you do not bring your best, you will not be able to achieve them. Goals should provide feedback on progress.*

Controlling Your Environment

Understanding Your Environment

Remember that Manhattan penthouse you can have, if you just erect the building according to my blueprints? Well, congratulations, you've decided to build it. You know, that means you're now going to need lots of money, a willing seller (not much available acreage in Manhattan), an architect, a team to help you market the building, construction people, and a good banker or two. Or three. A dozen.

And amassing and maintaining a team with the requisite relation-ships is just one of countless environmental factors you'll need to manage before you can start building that building.

Your goal—to build a building in NYC—is the *what*, and it's set. Environmental variables make up the *how*, and it's up to you to manage all those variables without losing sight of your ultimate goal. Regardless of the fact that the *how* usually comes after the goal has been created, the two are closely linked through feedback loops: progress feedback may just as likely indicate the need for environ-mental refinements as opposed to goal refinements.

Creating and maintaining an environment that is conducive to achieving your goals means three things:

1. That you have access to enabling people
2. That you have enabling resources
3. That you are in an enabling place

By *people*, I mean the relationships necessary to unlock access to crit-ical resources necessary to achieve your goal.

By *resources*, I mean access to the capital, in whatever form it takes—money, tools, intellectual property, or a combination thereof—to achieve your goal.

By *place*, I mean that you can physically take advantage of the opportunities, people, and resources needed to achieve your goal.

When I talk about environment, these are the things I am talking about. I'm not implying the finest digs, most expensive furniture, or priciest rent. I'm talking about being in a place where you have access to the people and resources to get things done.

By watching and adjusting these environmental variables, you remove obstacles from your path and make consistent progress toward your goal. You sow the seeds for Magic Moments.

"Uh-oh. Jase, don't tell me your whole model is predicated upon the assumption that I can wave a magic wand and magically get access to all the people, places, and things I need to become successful. That would be silly, naive, and childish!"

Yeah, that would be silly. I mean, if you had the power to conjure up people, places, and things with the wave of a wand . . . *huh*. Like, *wow*, you'd be bigger than Houdini, Copperfield, Blaine, and Angel all put together!

Come to think of it, having that ability sounds like it would be more awesome than silly. My plan wouldn't require naive assumptions as much as godlike control over your world. You'd be like a deity from a creation story, like one of those half-horse people in the sky who put fish in the sea, entombed their enemies in the mountains of Earth, turned unrequited lovers into the moon and stars, all that jazz. You and I would have to hang out. For *sure*.

Which reminds me: I seem to recall from those creation stories that we're all made in the image of those deities and all carry a divine spark within us. I know not *everyone's* religious—only 85 percent of Americans claimed a religion in 2008, according to the American Religious Identification Survey for that year—but if the divine spark thing is true, then maybe we can conjure these things . . . maybe because we're made in the image God, as opposed to being gods ourselves, we're like poor copies that just take a little more time and a lot more work than a quick flick of the wrist to do the conjuring. That's not such a silly thought, is it? That we could create things in this world, and that one of the things we can create is "the proper conditions" to create something bigger? You know, assuming we worked at it?

Come to think of it, that's not a silly notion at all.

Are You Rationalizing Your Environment?

You know what is silly? Thinking that you *can't* create anything. Thinking that you're a pinball being bopped around by forces greater than yourself with zero influence whatsoever to push back, change, move, resist, run, adapt, learn, grow, fight, conquer. *That's* silly. That's thinking that leads people to unnecessarily rationalize away their ability to control their own environments. To wit, take a look at the rationalizations that follow.

Rationalization #1: Seeking Authority

"I don't have the authority to get my job done."

The assumption behind this statement is that you cannot do the job without the authority to compel others to help you.

So what, I'm supposed to give you the formal authority to boss people around? Is that the kind of culture we all want to foster? The kind where people boss others around? I mean, as long as *you're* the boss, of course. Otherwise, forget it.

Yes, I'm being facetious.

Formal authority is only one of five different kinds of power you can use to "compel" others to help you. Others include various forms of influence, from the benign (being a respected person) to the manipulative (controlling resources), but I'm going to go out on a limb and say that if you're not sharp enough to figure out how to influence others into helping you beyond trying to push them around, you'd be a real terror with formal authority. Therefore, you get none.

Formal authority is like a loan from the bank. You'll get it when you no longer need it.

Rationalization #2: Relying on Existing Relationships

"I can't talk to *him*, I wouldn't know what to say!"

You need someone for your plans. You have no relationship with the person now. If you call her up, there are two potential outcomes: either you get what you want or you don't get what you want. If you don't get what you want, you're no worse off than you are now. This is what we call a "zero pressure situation."

If you're feeling pressure, then, even if you don't realize it, you should consider that you may be erecting unnecessary, artificial road-blocks for yourself. There are plenty of reasons why the conversation may be a bad idea . . . but if you get stuck on not knowing what to say, you keep yourself stuck on a point that doesn't even require a solution. "Hi, this is Jason Seiden. I have a program I want to tell you about, I think you'll find it interesting. Call me." That works! It's not brilliant, it will be ineffective much of the time, but if you put at least that much out there, you're at least in the game where interesting things can happen.

Rationalization #3: Staying Stuck in a Situation

"In order to make this happen, I'd need to live in a different city."

Then move.

"But I have a mortgage . . ."

Sell.

"But my friends are here . . ."

What, is there something about you that makes it impossible for you to make new friends?

"You're not taking this seriously!"

No, *you're* not taking it seriously. If your goal is that important to you and the resources and people you need to make it happen all exist elsewhere, then *go to where you need to be.* Don't sit around in the suburbs of Chicago and complain that you can't break into show business. Of course you can't, there's no show business here to break into. Do what my little sister did and move your butt to New York or L.A. And if you aren't willing to uproot yourself, then we need to get one thing out in the open right now: your goal is not to break into show business but to enjoy theater as a hobby while nurturing your relationships with current friends and family. If you're not willing to move, that's a de facto admission that your goal of stardom is less important than your goal of being comfortable. Which is OK—you can create Magic Moments and achieve career staying power just the same—if you're honest with yourself! Besides, if you don't think you could handle the challenge of moving to a new city, how do you suppose you would handle the insanity of all that stardom you think you want?

Rationalization #4: Staying Stuck on What Could Have Been

"If only I had invested that money in gold . . ."

If only I could tell the future, I could play the lottery and win! If only I had been born rich, this wouldn't be a problem! If only I'd bought that stock! Sold that bond! Answered that call! Sat in a different seat! Made the shot! Missed the bus! Taken the chance! Said no! Said yes! Kept my mouth shut!

Yes, if only you had more money. But you don't. So stop whining about it and let's figure out a way to get it for you.

Rationalization #5: Worrying About What Others Think

"I can't. She'd get mad."

Fantastic. I now know how to control you: get you to like me, and then threaten to get upset any time you do something I don't like. This process—using specific consequences to guide your behavior—is called operant conditioning. (If you don't like the name, blame B. F. Skinner.) In lay terms, when someone trains you to behave a certain way by alternatively threatening an emotional reaction and "rewarding" you with the removal of that threat, it's known as emotional manipulation, and it results in power. Over you. And no one's to blame for it but you.

Make the choice: your goal, or someone else's fleeting emotion.

Rationalization #6: Waiting for Everything to Be in Place First

"I don't know where I'll find the equipment. I can't even start talking to customers until I know for sure for certain for absolute that I can deliver."

Business is uncertain. On occasion, you'll need to make a promise without knowing how you'll keep your word. Not because you're lying or unethical but because you'll be asked to do something that's never been done before. That's life; embrace it. And hope that when you need it, the right equipment finds you . . . which it often does.

I distinctly remember skiing a run called Gandy Dancer at Mary Jane and having a rented ski pop off in the middle of a turn through the bumps. Because of the flex in the ski, it snapped up and caught me right beneath my kneecap; the impact was one of those sharp bites that makes you see stars.

I saw stars.

That was the day I discovered I was skiing outside the limits of the rental equipment, and I had to make a choice either to get out of the bumps or to start using skis better suited to my preferred conditions and terrain and my take-no-prisoners style. In talking to the pros at the base, I learned something surprising: my problem wasn't the skis as much as it was the boots and bindings. The equipment was finding me. Had I taken the attitude of "I can't ski bumps until I have all the 'right' gear," I would have wasted my money on skis I didn't need, and I would have created additional problems for myself because in skiing, like in many things in life, more advanced equipment is more difficult to use.

The lesson here for your career? Take things one step at a time. Do the best you can with what you've got. When you have an issue, look for a solution to that issue. (I didn't complain to the pros that I needed better gear; I explained what I was trying to do and the problem I was having.) When you solve problems, the support structure finds you.

Rationalization #7: Blaming Coworkers

"I have a coworker who is out to get me!"

Possible, but unlikely. I have met with many, many people who believed they had enemies who were out to get them. But rarely have I met anyone who said they got up in the morning and made a list of the people whose lives they hoped to ruin that day. More typical was that two people who didn't care for each other would zing each other out of a sense of tit-for-tat, both believing to have been victimized first by the other.

If you see yourself as having no enemies and treat people as friends rather than enemies, you will reduce opportunities for others to feel aggrieved by you, lowering the number of times people consider you an enemy and weakening their resolve when they do.

When you can look at coworkers and accept them as full, complex human beings who are neither all good nor all bad, and intepret their actions—both helpful and hurtful—with a benefit of doubt rather than judgment, then you can turn potential enemies into allies almost immediately.

Rationalization #8: Blaming Your Boss

"Sure, that works for a coworker, but what about when my enemy is my boss and he won't let me move up?"

OK, get ready, this is the only time you're going to hear me say this . . . I am an ardent proponent of making things work where you are, and an evangelist for personal responsibility . . . but assuming that you are right about this, and there's nothing you can do, then you are going to want to dust off your résumé.

There. I said it.

Now let me also say this: that should be your action of last, last resort. The odds of your toiling away for a monster without recourse are likely lower than you believe. More likely is that you are working for someone who was trained to think functionally about things like planning, budgeting, and staffing but never received instruction on the social aspects of management, such as how to hire, maintain a staff, give feedback, develop talent, negotiate for resources, and the like. Layer on top of this the strategic ambiguity many managers are required to grapple with, and you get a situation that can be frustrating but is not evil. You're going to need the Three Perspectives model to understand how to influence your boss. That model will help you see a path to assessing the true nature of the relationship and a way to fix it.

Read on, my friend!

Creating an Environment Conducive to Your Success

There are two ways to "control" your environment through adaption: the first is to accept your environment for what it is and enjoy the challenges it presents. Let's call this passive environing. The second is to constantly work to improve it. Let's call this active environing.

If you want to create Magic Moments, you'll need to know how to do both. You'll also need to know when to use one approach versus the other.

Passive Environing

Sometimes, you get lucky, and you find yourself in the right place at the right time. Rarely is the environment totally perfect, but Magic Moments don't require total perfection; they only require functional perfection. If the environment enables you to have a Magic Moment, then use passive environing to ensure that you don't disrupt the feast the universe is serving up just for you.

Have you ever been to dinner with friends where you were having such a great time that you overlooked the restaurant's poor service? Maybe your order came out wrong, but there was a great flow to the conversation and the vibe was so perfect that you didn't want to interrupt it by calling your server back over? In that moment, you were passively environing. When passively environing, you will doubtlessly notice aspects of your physical surroundings that could be changed or improved upon, and you will have to weigh the potential benefit of fixing them against the potential cost of interrupting the current environment. To determine whether or not to fiddle with a passively managed environment, ask yourself these four questions about a considered change:

- ► Will the change improve more than just aesthetics?
- ► Will the change improve conditions for someone other than myself?
- ► Will execution of the change require my direct involvement?
- ► Can the change be made unobtrusively?

If you answer no to any one of these questions, then passively environ; try to avoid disrupting the flow.

Active Environing

What about the times when things don't fall into place? When the universe conspires against you? Sometimes you need to take matters into your own hands.

Several years ago, I conducted a training session for a client. The facility we met in had a mini-museum to showcase some of the company's products, and someone had thought it would be a good idea to conduct the program in the museum. Which would have been fine had I been using the projector and speaking from a podium. The problem was, I wasn't. I was interacting with the group, encouraging group participation and small-team discussions, and the room wasn't set up for that. For one thing, there was no lighting; all the lights were trained on the walls, where the products and photographs and displays were, leaving a big dark spot in the middle where the people were. For another thing, the acoustics were dampened to facilitate privacy for groups touring the place. And finally, the place was cavernous. The energy of our little group of twenty quickly dissipated into the ether.

The training program was scheduled to last two and a half days. An hour into day one, everyone knew the arrangement wouldn't work. By lunch, the head of the division and I had scouted an alternative location. When the food arrived, before people started eating, we stopped the program.

"OK, who's up for an adventure?"

The division head told the group what we were thinking. A cheer went up, and immediately our group of twenty men and women started folding up the tables, stacking the chairs, and dragging everything—including the food tray—across the hall into a room that was oddly shaped, had no whiteboard, and was so cramped with the tables in it that we ended up leaving half of them leaning against the wall in the hallway. (Imagine a parade led by people in sport jackets and dresses wheeling large, round banquet tables down the hall, and followed by others lugging heaping tablecloths, dragging screeching stacks of chairs, and carrying precariously balanced stacks of boxes, and you get the picture.) We made it work somehow, and we had fun doing it.

Had we tried passive environing, the program would have failed. People would not have been able to hear, they would have been bored, and they would have tuned out. As it was, the room we moved into was too hot and too cramped to be comfortable, but because it was a choice we made actively—and because we knew the alternative was worse!—the location of our training became part of the program's story and therefore part of its success. We didn't merely talk about Magic Moments during that event; we created one.

Know Whether to Actively or Passively Environ

Could these two situations have gone another way? Certainly. Nothing is a given. Managing the environment is how we set the stage for a Magic Moment, but while environing can maximize the odds of fostering a Magic Moment, no environmental change can guarantee one will occur. Even at Disney World, famous for its Magic Moment–enabling environment, people sometimes leave unhappy and unfulfilled.

Often you can determine whether to actively or passively environ based on a single, most important environmental variable. If you ask yourself what the most important environmental variable is—what is the one thing you most need for success—the answer can dictate which form of environing to use.

For instance, when I am facilitating a training event, the most important factor for success is generally my ability to hold participants' attention. Cell phones ringing, laptops announcing new e-mails, people constantly walking in and out, people engaged in activities unrelated to the immediate discussion—these are the things that will most inhibit a training cohort from achieving a Magic Moment. So I actively manage these interruptions out of the environment as best I can: I remind people to turn off their phones. I move through the group when I speak, forcing people to look around and making it difficult for people in the back to tune out. I take short breaks every ninety minutes, which is consistently when I see groups' energy levels flag, unless the group itself says they want to keep going. I refuse to hand out my presentation notes ahead of time, sending them out to groups afterward instead, to serve as reminders; this forces people to stay in the moment and keeps them together as a group. I present information informally and in bursts, intercutting lessons with frequent human-to-human interaction to keep people on their toes. Finally, I request rooms that are slighty too small for the group, since different behavioral norms take over when people are in close proximity to one another as compared to when they are spread out.

Beyond this, I generally passively environ. For instance, if I am speaking to a group of fewer than eighty people or so, and a computer or projector is not ready the moment I need it, I don't use it. I know how to convey my information orally, or with a whiteboard, and what I lose in doing it low-tech style is negligible when weighed against the loss of time and attention I would suffer while trying to get a piece of technology to work. This changes only when the group size gets larger because of the power technology has to amplify a message and help fill a room.

The Folly That Active Environing Is Necessarily Better

Don't be in such a hurry to put your personal stamp on things that you insist on actively environing even when handed a ready-made Magic Moment. Many young careerists who are not yet familiar with what will create Magic Moments at work make this mistake. I made this mistake. Frequently, this mistake comes in the form of believing that you have to forge your own path and "make it on your own terms." Really, all that "making it on your own terms" means is that you choose to accept help from some people and not others. Specifically, you accept help from those who validate your struggle, and reject help from those who hand you a ready-made solution. Of course, that's not what you tell yourself; you tell yourself that the people trying to help are imposing their will on you against your wishes and that the people enabling your struggle are offering you a way out.

The reason you have it backward is because your ego is involved in the decision. When that happens, you're working against yourself; you're choosing active environing when you should be choosing passive environing, and in so doing you're creating a situation where the small Magic Moments you create for yourself come at the expense of bigger, more rewarding Magic Moments you could be creating if you took advantage of the tools that were being handed to you.

Keep your ego out of it, zero in on what's most important, and go. Americans especially tend to engage in a bit of hero-worship with regard to people who successfully engage in active environing. We forget that even the quintessential American hero—think Marshal Will Kane, the gun-slinging Western sheriff from *High Noon*—first asked every member of the town for help, some of them twice, before going out to fight the bad guys alone. When offered help, take it; passive environing takes a whole lot less energy than active environing.

The Relationship Between Goals and Environment

Setting a proper environment creates points of connection between your goals and your environment, some of them surprising, such as how your environment can make feedback easier or more difficult to obtain. The more variables you have in your environment that you do not control, the more uncertain the feedback you receive will be, as it will be difficult to know what you are receiving feedback about. On the other hand, the more tightly you control your environment, the more ambiguous the feedback you receive will be, as people try to force the limited feedback channels that exist to serve their own needs.

For instance, if you were to take control of your career path by signing up for a coveted international project that would put you in line for a promotion, the moment you win the position, you should expect the quantity and quality of feedback you get to change. For one thing, winning a spot on a coveted project signals to your peers that you are good, politically astute, and maybe both. For another thing, management now knows that you have some career ambition. In both cases, you will have limited the number of feedback channels coming into you—peers can no longer trust that you won't use what they tell you for your own advancement, and management can no longer hand you information because they need to test your ability to reach the *next* level. In both cases, the feedback you receive will become increasingly ambiguous: there will be times when you won't be sure if you're getting the whole story from your peers, and there will be times when you won't be sure if management has overlooked you or is testing you.

Another way in which your goals and environment interact is through the way in which you shape your environment: if your process fosters within others a desire to help you, then you not only are going to be able to more readily get the people and resources you need to be successful, but you will also be able to push the line between what's real and what's tough outward. This is why it's often difficult to ask, outright, for help in a political environment: asking a direct question in a political environment signals a political naïveté. So while your request is an invitation to help, the way in which you make that request—the blunt process you use—discourages people from helping you because your lack of savvy could land them into trouble if you're not careful.

As best you can, look two steps out to understand how changes in your environment will ripple out and affect your goal, and how those changes will ripple back to create new environmental challenges. This will help you shape the environment you have today into the one you'll need tomorrow.

IN THIS SECTION

▶ **How are your goals and the environment linked?** *Goals are the* what. *The environment is the* how. *Feedback links goals with the environment; when you receive feedback, you need to determine if you have an environmental misalignment,* *or whether the problem is that your goal is too tough or not realistic.*

▶ **What eight statements diminish your ability to control your environment?** *(1) "I don't have the authority to get my job done." (2) "I wouldn't know what to say." (3) "I'd need to live in a different city." (4) "If only I had more money." (5) "I can't, she'd get mad." (6) "I don't have the right equipment." (7) "My coworker is out to get me." (8) "My enemy is my boss and he won't let me move up."*

▶ **What is the difference between active and passive environing?** *Active environing means shaping your environment to suit your needs. Passive environing means shaping your attitude and approach to suit the environment. Either can be appropriate, depending on the situation.*

The Winner's Attitude

Protect Your Mind

To paraphrase Elie Wiesel, author, Nobel Peace Prize winner, and Holocaust survivor: protect your mind; it's all you've got.

The question, of course, is *how*? I mean, don't we protect our minds every day? Isn't that what we do when we watch the news—

try to understand our world better so we can make better decisions? Isn't that what we do when we live vicariously through others—try to extrapolate how we would behave in similar situations so that we're prepared for them if they ever come our way? Isn't that why we read, blog, watch, pray, critique . . . engage? These things are enlightening! Enriching! Uplifting! When Karl Marx called religion the "opiate of the masses," he *clearly* did not understand that religion is how we find inner peace and expand our minds! Ditto talk radio and the cinematic arts! C'mon, people!

As we saw in the section on goals, our minds can be easily influenced in very subtle, insidious ways that we are often blind to. In doing what we believe to be wisest, we open ourselves to what we believe to be good sources of information and turn off what we consider bad information. But depending on the perspective we use to view that information, we may or may not perceive the information giver's true motives, and so we may inadvertently open ourselves up to negative influence, especially if the information giver's perspective is broader than our own.

Sometimes it's fun to allow others to shape our interpretations of what's going on, sometimes not so much. Watching a magician perform a trick? Fun. Watching a comedian? Also fun. Advocating a political or religious "morality" that leads us to become hypocrites when our leaders turn out to be con men? Not fun. Funding a good idea that later becomes an existential threat to life on earth? Again, not fun.

Our problem is not that we don't know that the information we get from others is slanted or biased—we expect that. Our problem is that we don't understand that the bias we see is a ruse. Like a good magician's trick, biased information makes you think one thing, while concealing its real intention, but unlike a magician's trick, there is no reveal, and no resetting the stage back to its original form. We are never told that what we have seen is an illusion.

I have a good friend in the television business—in the news business, actually. He used to work for a station that let him say whatever he wanted during his reports, but he was severely limited in what stories he was allowed to report on. By measuring the bias of the news by counting the number of times positive or negative language was used, this station could claim neutrality. Yet it was advocating its particular political view by controlling what news was given airtime. The well-intended loyal viewers who didn't catch on unintentionally opened themselves up to subtle and powerful forms of influence.

I am often asked, regarding the structural behavioral interviews I use to assess executive talent, how I handle it if someone tries to pull the wool over my eyes. I must say, I find this question odd. I expect *everyone* to try to influence me. In fact, I want to see that attempt—if you are going to be running a major company, you had better be working to convert everyone you meet into an ally for your organization. Now, just because people try to influence me doesn't make them bad. It just means they have control over their perspective and want me to see things their way. Even if the goal is self-preservation, having a parochial worldview is not evil. There need not be a conspiracy for people to want to influence me. However, neither is there an obligation on my part to submit to their views or refrain from acknowledging what I see to be going on. But I have to be operating in the right perspective to be able to do this.

There is a quirk in our human nature that makes it difficult to reconcile conflicting feedback about others' intentions. That quirk is that our brains are able to hold two competing beliefs simultaneously—for instance, one belief, based on interpersonal clues, that says, yes, I should trust this person, and another belief, based on cold, hard evidence, that says, no, I shouldn't—without reconciling them. Then we march headlong into an impending disaster we see coming. When forced to reconcile these competing beliefs, our brains may do so, but they just as easily may not, in which case we get stressed out but don't do anything. This mental quirk is called cognitive dissonance, and it's one more example of how, as amazing and awe-inspiring an organ as the brain is, it truly sucks in some very fundamental ways.

If we're going to protect our attitude and mind-set, we've got to know and accept that we're dealing with an imperfect organ. Only then can we demystify how we process information and build better filters. And the bottom line is, what we've got is to carbon systems what a buggy operating system is to a computer. We can't assume that everything we think is correct; sometimes we need to accept that what's happening in our minds is the result of a program crashing— the mental equivalent of the blue screen of death or a divide-by-zero command.

(Have you ever needed to clear your mind? Yes? That's people-talk for rebooting.)

Get a Sense of the Human Condition

How often have you had a friend come to you, noticeably upset, and say something to the effect of "I can't believe my boss! I was totally calm! I did everything right! I treated that conniving, mean-spirited jerk with the utmost respect! I didn't raise my voice one bit! I was as relaxed during our conversation as I am now! And he *still* refused to give me the 50 percent raise I demanded!" At this point you look at your buddy, who is still seething with negative emotion, and you wonder many things. Like how is it possible that one person can be so totally devoid of self-awareness? Or which approach would be the most effective in helping him right now—staying silent, recording him so he can hear himself, or taking a two-by-four upside his head? Or why is he still talking about himself? *Dude, I don't care.*

At about this point you look at your buddy and, if you say anything at all, you say, "You're not being serious right now, are you?"

How often has the friend in the situation been you, and you've sat there, justifying your whiny behavior by crying, "Of course I'm serious! Don't you understand? This is *different*!"

Yes, different. Different because your brain is blind to its own problems, so it can't see how it's actually identical to everyone else's. You're like a zebra that can't see its own stripes and thinks it's a horse. Meanwhile, the rest of the world shakes its collective head.

Travel Beyond the Obvious

My dad once told me a riddle that helped clarify the problem with the human condition for me. It goes like this:

Two chimney sweeps come down a chimney. One's face is covered with soot; the other's is clean. Who washes his face? Answer: the guy with the clean face, because when they look at each other, the guy with the clean face sees the other guy's face is dirty and assumes his is, too. Meanwhile, the guy with the dirty face assumes his own face is clean when he sees his partner's clean face.

Hang on, there's more. Let's try this again: two chimney sweeps come down a chimney. One's face is covered with soot; the other's is clean. Who washes his face? Answer: the guy with the dirty face. See, the guy with the clean face says, "I'm going to wash my face," to which the guy with the dirty face says, "Why?" In the conversation that follows, they figure out what's what, and Mr. Sooty Cheeks goes to wash up.

OK, one last time. Try to get it right this time. Here we go: two chimney sweeps come down a chimney. One's face is covered with soot; the other's is clean. Who washes his face? Answer: both of them. The idea of a chimney sweep coming out of a chimney with a clean face is absurd.

The point is, the human condition is capable of suspending disbelief, which can make it difficult to interpret even the most obvious clues, as highlighted by the riddle.

Your buddy complaining about his boss? He's like one of the chimney sweeps from the first version of the riddle, blind to his own condition. He looks only at his boss's reaction and ignores the fact that what his boss sees could look much different. Also like the chimney sweep, it may take an outside voice to help him realize what he should have known up front: that his initial interpretation that someone could have come out of the situation "clean" was ridiculous from the start.

This is the essence of the human condition.

What a mess.

I hope what these examples make clear is that cultivating a winner's attitude is not simply a matter of sticking a poster on the wall and then working harder to cultivate it. The clean-faced chimney sweep doesn't solve anything by scrubbing his face harder!

We need to go deeper. We need to get to the core of what drives us so we can rise above our human condition and see the world for what it really is. If we are going to create Magic Moments, we need to be in total control, not just of our external environment but of ourselves, too.

Results, Behavior, and Perspective, Meet Focus, Persistence, and Openness

Results are driven by behaviors. Behaviors are driven by perspective.

Much of the time, we think about the results we want to achieve. When we want new results, we think tactically, focusing on a task list or the speed with which we move through tasks, or strategically focusing on profits or risk or brand equity. Changes made at the results level show up in the numbers column of a plan—the goal doesn't change, the methods don't change. Only the outcomes change. This type of thinking deals with what we see. The clean-faced chimney sweep who goes and washes up after seeing his soot-covered pal is engaged in outcome-based thinking.

The second level of thinking looks one step past the results and determines, through logic, how to alter future results by engaging in a different set of behaviors. This thinking is proactive and logical and, if practiced with enough repetition and under specific circumstances, can be used to create new behaviors that, planned properly, will lead to superior results. For example, we know that if we lift a heavy bar thirty times, a few times a week, our arms will get bigger. If our goal is bigger arms, and we engage in this bar-lifting behavior repeatedly, we achieve our goal. Changes made at the activity level appear in plans as changes to activity line items and indirectly affect outcomes.

But, anyone who has ever made and broken a New Year's resolution, struggled to give something up for Lent, or failed to keep a promise to do better next time—against the very best of best intentions—has run smack into the core limitation of a behavioral focus: it's not sticky. It takes a lot a lot a lot of repetitions before behavioral conditioning begins to stick. You have to get the rewards and punishments just right. Heck, some people graduate from college and still don't know how to study, even after sixteen years of practice!

The stickiest, most effective type of thinking occurs at the perspective level. Changing your behavior sticks much faster when your underlying worldview supports the new behavior in which you are trying to engage.

Take a smoker. (For sake of argument, I am going to assume this particular smoker is aware of the risks associated with lighting up.) Why doesn't she quit? It's not like there aren't any alternative ways she can satisfy that nicotine craving! No, she doesn't quit because she holds a worldview that makes quitting unnecessary. Maybe she believes she's going to get hit by a bus long before cancer sets in. Maybe she believes she won't get sick because her parents smoked and lived into their nineties. Maybe she doesn't believe the hype. Maybe she works for a cigarette company and doesn't know what she'd do if the company went away, and this is her small, distorted way of trying to create staying power.

She may not even be consciously aware of how her worldview affects her decision to continue to smoke. She may only know that when she tries to do what she knows she should, the behavior doesn't stick. To make it stick, she needs to attack her worldview. Her belief system. Her perspective.

This is what the winner's attitude is all about: acknowledging that victory requires a holistic approach that solves our problems at the source. Perspective drives behaviors, and behaviors drive outcomes? OK, then if we want to win, we've got to control the entire chain: we need to be focused on results, we need to be persistent in practicing new behaviors, and we need to be open to new perspectives. Gaining control over these three areas will help us create more Magic Moments.

Focus

The world throws a lot of stuff at you. Big stuff. Somehow, the more clearly you see your goal and the more you fix your environment, the more tempting the stuff is that will get thrown at you. It's like a video game that gets harder as you get better, except it's real, there's no reset button, and the possible outcomes are infinitely more complex. And for that reason, the quest for Magic Moments requires increasingly intense focus as you move forward, as the variables affecting your goals, environment, and mental state multiply in number, type, and complexity.

To achieve a Magic Moment, you need to do more than keep track of a great number of variables, and you need to be able to concentrate on all of them without losing singularity of focus on your goal. You need to have such a clear image in your head of what you want that you can see, in your mind's eye, how all the pieces fit together. Focus means more than the mental discipline to keep your eyes trained on what's in front of you; it means keeping the vision of where you're going superimposed atop whatever it is you see in front of you. (Personally, this is my challenge. I'm a door opener. I'm wired to see connections, so, to me, opening another door doesn't seem like a lack of focus; it seems like a natural extension of a given direction. I have used others on my team to help me in this area.)

A lot of gurus like to talk about the power of focus, and with good reason. Whether you're a New Ageist who believes an invisible force becomes unlocked through focus, or an Old Schooler who believes in concentrating your critical-thinking skills on a single problem, focus helps. A lot.

Tough business problems require concentration. They have moving parts that are not readily apparent, that cannot be grasped with only a cursory review of things. To solve these problems, you need an opportunity to make connections between disparate pieces of data, to draw connections, to see trends, to get frustrated, to experiment using old information in new ways, to seek out how to learn new information to solve old problems. No focus, no Magic Moment. No Magic Moment, no success. If you're unpracticed, a warning: you'll find focusing about as easy as doing a crossword puzzle in your head and memorizing the answers as you go.

Persistence

How many people escape their jobs in hopes of finding something more suitable for themselves, get excited about the new gig, lose the excitment shortly after starting, repeat? What's funny to me is, when I've lost something, I always retrace my steps rather than go look in places I've never been before. If you lost your enthusiasm at your current job, why would you think you'd find it at a new one? Sometimes there is a good reason for this loss of enthusiasm, like a new boss or a change in responsibilities, but often the answer is less concrete, having to do with a feeling of not making the most of one's talents. Problem is, if I can't make things work here, I won't be able to get them to work in the new place, either. That new job will hold my interest only for as long as it remains a sparkly, shiny object, maybe longer if I luck out and find a mentor, and then I'll tire of it and move on, racking up yet another too-short stint for my résumé.

Success comes to the person who doesn't just outlast adversity but whose stubborn persistence ensures that she masters the behaviors needed to achieve success on her own accord.

Of course, there is a fine line between being persistent and being a stubborn ass, if there is a line at all:

If you fail ten thousand times and then succeed, the world will celebrate your persistence. If you fail ten thousand times and die penniless before your epic win finds you, the world will mock you at your grave. Unfortunately, you won't know which path you're on until you get through those ten thousand failures.

Daunting as that may sound, I would encourage you to go for it and get those ten thousand attempts under your belt, even at the risk of being mocked. Who cares what the critics in the cheap seats are saying anyway? Didn't we just get through a whole section about blocking out bad influences?!

If you are persistent in your pursuit of Magic Moments, dogmatically refining your environment and tenaciously clinging to your goal, a good number of people will call you a stubborn ass. A good number of *those* people will be right. If you don't have the stomach for the punches you are bound to take en route to your goal, you probably should close this book right now and give it to someone who does. Persistence takes personal courage, the kind no one can help you with. You're going to need to take a hard look at yourself in the mirror and decide for yourself if you've got the mettle to get back up every time the world beats you down to your knees.

And rest assured, you will get beaten down. Anyone who fails ten thousand times does. Eventually, after it has happened enough, you will begin to doubt your commitment to your goal, you will lose confidence in your ability to control your environment, and you will start to mock your ability to focus as nothing more than the ability to take another punch. You will wonder if you will ever achieve the level of behavioral excellence required to succeed.

That's when you will need a persistent attitude.

Openness

Let's go back to my perfect day and replay it from a closed, impatient perspective:

I get a call one night from Todd, inviting me to come skiing with him the next day. In reality, the invitation amounts to an obligation, since he knows I'm captive and have no plans other than to ski. When I show up on the mountain, I can see immediately by the company that I'm way in over my head. I wonder briefly if Todd's plan isn't to have me suffer some sort of "accident," and I quickly start thinking about anything I may have done to piss him off.

We hit the mountain, and sure enough, the crew does everything in their power to ditch me. Not just once or twice, either, but on every run. I'm racing to keep up, but some of the terrain we're skiing is just plain terrifying, and I've got to slow down. I can't count how many times I find myself lost. Even the weather is against me! Forty degrees in March is T-shirt weather; have you ever wiped out skiing at thirty-five miles per hour through spring slush in a T-shirt? My entire left side, from shoulder to wrist to ribs to hip, is one giant raspberry by the end of the day. And the best part: the day costs me a minor fortune in repairs to my equipment and leaves my brand-new pants with a major gash in them (courtesy of some exposed rock). Just great. And I'm supposed to get excited by a so-called perfect turn here and there? Please.

Needless to say, an open perspective—a willingness to find adventure in adversity, to not sweat the small stuff, to be willing to absorb small costs for big wins—is critical to building and maintaining a winner's attitude.

To hold an open perspective, it helps to be aware of and accepting of the human condition—foibles and all. When you deny the realities of your human condition, you blind yourself to critical information and set yourself back to being the chimney sweep in the riddle. When you can accept who you are—shortcomings and all—it becomes easier to see the ridiculousness in the idea that you might come through with a clean face, so to speak. You become more willing to hear the truth in the observations others make about you. You won't necessarily be happy about it, mind you, but it does get easier.

There is one big thing you can do to help open up your perspective and give yourself more patience with the human condition, and that is to sort of meditate. I say sort of meditate because I don't necessarily mean sit on the floor in a candlelit room with your eyes closed. Unless that works for you. I mean the idea more generically: engage in behaviors that help you quiet your mind. For me, it's often running, or working on projects around the house. In a day filled with mental acrobatics, there's something wonderfully liberating about spending a few hours engaged in a mindless, even tedious, physical activity. I encourage you to find your own form of sort of meditation and use that time to allow your subconscious to work through issues, because the times when you turn your brain—and by extension, your filters, judgments, and assumptions—off, you are at your most open and patient.

Put It All Together

"What's all this got to do with me keeping my job?"

You're a manager, and you've got to trim your budget. You look over your staff. You've got a bunch of folks who are average performers, and then you've got this one kid who's . . . different. In a good way. He's giving it everything he's got, and, more than that, he's operating at a level above everyone else. He has a winner's attitude. While the others bug you about how to earn promotions, he comes to you to test his hypothesis about the connection between some part of your workflow and the results the team is posting. He knows the path to a promotion, but he doesn't come into your office to talk about it; he just walks it. His actions demonstrate that he understands the power of relationships, the need to move a bit nonlinearly toward the team's ultimate goal, and an unflinching openness. As tough as things can get, this guy doesn't miss a chance to celebrate someone's success, and he does it genuinely. This guy not only has Magic Moments, but he creates the conditions for others to have them.

Is *this* the guy you're going to move out?

Or is this guy the type of employee you're going to hold onto and try to hire more of?

Now do you see the connection?

Not quite? Let me put it more plainly: that guy has staying power. He is resilient without even trying. He supports everyone else, celebrates their successes, and, in so doing, becomes the one his manager is most likely to support. What this has to do with your job is *be that guy.*

WHAT YOU LEARNED

► **How do I know if I'm protecting my mind-set or exposing it to bad influences?** *If you are listening to another person, you are exposing your mind to potentially bad influences. This is not a conspiracy theory become manifest. This is organizational* *dynamics: every organization, even an organization of one, has something to sell, even if just an opinion. This is true for every institution, every organization, every person in your life, no matter how close they are. Everyone has his own worldview and his own set of personal interests, and you should expect everyone is trying to influence you for their own benefit. By the way, this does not make them evil, only human.*

▶ **Why isn't it enough to focus on engaging in the right behaviors?** *Outcomes are driven by behaviors. Behaviors are driven by perspective. Want to make a lasting behavioral change? Modify your perspective first. That will lead to new behaviors and new outcomes.*

▶ **What are the three elements of a positive attitude?** *Focus, persistence, and openness. You cannot force success!*

▶ **How can I spot others at work who have the right attitude?** *The person with the correct mind-set doesn't need to talk about things; his actions speak for him.*

PART 2

Reinforcing the Winner's Attitude Through the Three Perspectives

IN THIS SECTION

- ▶ What does courage feel like?
- ▶ How does fear affect career development?

Our human condition leaves us prone to errors in judgment when crafting goals, shaping our environment, and even holding onto a positive mind-set—errors we are frequently blind to. Magic Moments offer us a vision of what life feels like when we rise above these problems. The rest of the book focuses on how to master the most complicated element of the Magic Moment: perspective.

The right perspective is fundamental to success. Without changing a single fact, a new perspective can create a whole new story that changes everything. If the first part of the book gave us the model for success, then this part gives us the tools for actualizing that model. In the chapters that follow, we will anticipate the obstacles people are likely to face in their attempts to create Magic Moments and provide tools—primarily in the form of new perspectives—for overcoming those obstacles.

That obstacle, actually. Singular. Because when we get right down to it, the various problems people face are really all different manifestations of the same thing: fear.

The Courageous Mind Versus the Fearful Mind

At the very core of the human condition is the choice to face issues or hide from them. Facing issues means being open, inquisitive, and vulnerable in an ego-free kind of way. Hiding from them means engaging in avoidance behavior, blame, or redirection. It's fight or flight on a conceptual level! And, as the following story of the day my younger daughter was born illustrates, this choice exists on a primal, cellular level outside the scope of conscious thought.

On the surface, this story has nothing to do with work, but stick with me: since emotions are universal, the way we handle them is the same no matter if we are in the woods, the office, the house, or the delivery room. By improving your ability to draw wisdom from disparate, seemingly unrelated sources, you improve your ability to tap into your common genius, expanding the mental library of experiences you can call upon to solve work-related problems.

When my wife and I went into the hospital Sunday night and the doctors told us what was going on, we were a little scared. My wife's uterus had clotted after a prior bleeding episode in such a way that our daughter wasn't getting enough nutrients anymore, and carrying her to term might result in a miscarriage. The doctors wanted the baby out immediately. We spent the night in the hospital, and the next day prepped for delivery.

My wife received an epidural, but it wasn't working well. Only one side of her was numbed; the other side was excruciating. Having been through this process once before, we knew something out of the ordinary was going on. When we called the nurse to check my wife, she came with too many people and too much equipment; the arriving entourage provided confirmation that something was not as it should be. The nurse took some measurements and then said she wanted to take the pressure off of the baby during contractions . . . *pressure?* I thought. That's when I looked up at the heart monitor and saw that the baby's heart rate would fall precipitously with each contraction. I didn't say anything out loud, but I was pretty sure that the umbilical cord was wrapped around the baby's neck. The contractions were strangling the baby. The nurse said that with a small baby, sometimes the contractions could put undue stress on the baby's head, too— which did nothing to alleviate my concerns. Suddenly the doctor came in, breathing hard. He made an offhand comment about being out of shape, that the run from his office to the delivery room wasn't so long that he should be out of breath from it. I joked with him and kept a steady hold on my wife, but inside I couldn't help thinking: *Why was he running? What's the rush? What do these people all know that they're not saying?!* Something was definitely off.

After a minute of checking the monitors, the doctor saw something that made him fly into action. Fly. I don't know what he had been looking for or what he saw, but he interrupted himself mid-sentence to ask me and the head nurse to roll my wife from her side to her back so that he could check things out firsthand. That's when all hell broke loose.

My daughter was birthing herself. The look of shock on our faces when we saw this couldn't be hidden. Unfortunately, my wife happened to be looking at us—myself, the doctor, and the nurse—just at that moment when the shock hit our faces. There was no time to explain to her what was going on; all she knew was that something was wrong, that there was too much pain, and that the people around her were scared. The doctor told her not to push, yet he wasn't moving for a C-section. My wife could only imagine the reason. I stroked her hair and said, "I'm here, Vanessa. I'm right here." The doctor asked for clamps: "Bring me the clamps. Forget your prep; get me those clamps now!" He was as calm as anyone could be under the circumstances and handled things well, but there was no masking the seriousness of the situation. The nurses were a whirlwind of action. I held on to my wife, told her everything would be OK, and watched in dread as the doctor worked to unwind the umbilical cord from around the baby's neck. My wife remained beside herself in pain, even after the successful birth.

That was the day I froze. My daughter—who turned out to be healthy and fine—was already at the scales being weighed, and I still couldn't move. Not until the doctor asked me, "Dad, don't you want to grab your camera?" did I think about doing anything.

What Courage Feels Like

Had I not experienced that day in the delivery room, I doubt I would have appreciated just how debilitating fear can be, or how insidiously it can take over. I've been caught in a riptide, lost in a foreign country, and cornered by armed muggers twice; never did I lose control or not come out OK through my own efforts. And that's the thing: courage isn't a conscious thing. Consciously, courage feels exactly the same as fear. At least, initially. You could be lost in the woods, toe-to-toe with an intimidating boss, smelling smoke in your house, or looking at your daughter's blue face, and the feeling is exactly the same: what you're feeling at that moment is fear.

Fear's Impact at Work

I learned a lot from my experience in the delivery room that day, and what I learned helps me at work every day. I learned that having a vision of the future is insufficient planning, because when things go awry, and that vision goes poof, you may be left with nothing. I learned that a learning orientation is a must if you are going to get accurate process feedback in a novel situation. (I didn't know how to read the monitors, so I had to find other things to pay attention to in order to get the feedback I needed.) I also learned that access to outside help is a *must*, because if fear does take over, you can get locked out of your own thinking process without even knowing it. And finally, I learned that the biggest difference between this moment and other times when I've felt afraid was that this time, I allowed myself to entertain a feeling of being out of control.

Unfortunately, people are quite good at reinforcing feelings of being out of control. This is not unique to delivery rooms. People have been expressing such feelings relative to their work so frequently and for so long that the idea shapes the very fabric of our corporate culture. Institutions such as labor unions, songs such as Bruce Springsteen's "Born in the U.S.A." and The Police's "Synchronicity II," and movies such as *Office Space* and even *The Matrix* all tap into a common and accepted theme of powerlessness. And when this lack of control leads to inaction and then to fear, problems arise: fear of the unknown freezes people as they try to create objectives. Fear of being disliked or lonely keeps them from taking ownership of their environment. Fear of failure makes it tough for them to get in control of their mind-set, and from there it becomes a vicious cycle, resulting in self-imposed limitations, rationalizations, and permanent pockets of ignorance, where their inability to engage with their environment prevents them from understanding their world and taking appropriate action.

This section of the book is all about enabling Magic Moments by giving you a perspective about your work that puts you in control and eliminates fear. When you are 100 percent focused and 100 percent committed to the task at hand, there is no space in your psyche for anything else; fear has no doorway in. Whether you are monitoring your objective, managing your environment, or adjusting your mindset, Magic Moments can give you something to do, something within your control to focus on, that will help keep fear at bay.

The Three Perspectives Model

Now, we could also rely on courage to help us directly intervene to fill those pockets of fear. But calling upon courage means that you are face-to-face with your fears at a time when you may not be prepared to deal with them, and as I learned in the delivery room, courage won't always show up in that moment, even if you're the type of person who expects it to. Given my training, expertise, and experience, I think a better approach is to help you understand your world and know what to expect, so your need for courage is less.

The Three Perspectives model I use to help do this is based on a *Harvard Business Review* article written by R. L. Katz in the mid-1950s entitled "Skills of an Effective Administrator." Half a century later—despite six years of studying management theory in the world's most prestigious business institutions, researching for consulting engagements at some of the world's most successful companies, and reading countless books on the subject—I have yet to find anything more powerful than Katz's approach.

In short, I maintain that you can view work through one of three lenses: a functional lens, a social lens, or a political lens. And while the typical career progression includes an evolution through these perspectives, from functional to social to political, it is also true that you will interact with others regularly whose primary perspective is different from your own, and that by improving your ability to anticipate their needs based on their perspective, you will improve your ability to create Magic Moments and achieve lasting, meaningful staying power.

WHAT YOU LEARNED

▶ **What does courage feel like?** *Fear.*

▶ **How does fear affect career development?** *Fear creates a vicious mental cycle in which feelings of powerlessness become self-imposed limitations, which in turn stop people from doing the things they need to do to begin gaining control over their environment.*

5

Functional, Social, and Political

IN THIS SECTION

► What is the top skill necessary to achieve Magic Moments at work and succeed in your career?
► What are the three phases of career development?
► What is an example of an activity that when viewed from the first perspective seems like a good idea but when viewed from a higher-level perspective can be seen as harmful to career development?

Let's Rewire Your Brain

If you think the knowledge you've learned in class (and on the job and from performance reviews) is enough to help you succeed at work, you are one-third correct and two-thirds flat-out wrong.

What you get in school is functional ability—the ability to take direction and go do something with it. Excelling at this level assumes an authority figure, such as a teacher, as well as a formal structure in which to operate, such as a classroom of a given size, a school year of a given length, and tests of a particular type and frequency.

Not addressed in the classroom—and what doesn't seem to be learned on the playground anymore, either—are social and political abilities, such as the ability to play nicely in the sandbox and the ability to understand what drives the social pecking order and how to affect it in the absence of rules and structure.

The reason you need these two additional abilities is because without them, you see only one-third of your work issues, leaving two-thirds of your issues shrouded in darkness, outside of your control, and prone to fear-based interpretations. I don't want this to be you.

I must admit, the first time someone suggested that I accept politics as a reality of life, my reaction was, "Why, you dried-up old man, don't you dare expect that just because you caved in to your lesser nature that I will, too!" I still feel that way. I'm an idealist, and I think there is a better way to run a business than what we've got today. But to get there, we have to start from where we are today, and where are today is a world filled with dried-up old men who have caved. You can't approach business with the naïveté of a Pollyanna, who believes everything will be perfect because a textbook says it *should* be that way, and expect to get very far. Such is the attitude of a functionally minded individual. Keep the idealism, but ditch the ignorance about how the world looks from a social or political perspective. Understanding these two perspectives is imperative if you are going to get anything done.

From the functional perspective, the social and political perspectives can look not just foreign but somewhat evil. From what I have seen as a consultant, people's understanding of politics is usually based more on pockets of ignorance—presumptions, rationalizations, and fear—than on real information. People with a functional perspective tend to overuse their functional perspective, and their unwillingness to build an understanding of the other two perspectives inhibits their ability to correctly assess situations, frame expectations, and create ideal solutions.

Take the following statements, which, as colorful as they are, are pretty typical in corporate America, from what I can tell:

▶ "She's so narrow-minded that she rejects all my attempts to help her!"
▶ "If everyone just did their jobs, none of these problems would exist!"
▶ "He's a moron."
▶ "My boss refuses to give me the tools I need to do my job."
▶ "I do all the work, and he wants all the credit!"

If we take a closer look, it turns out each of these statements is clearly indicative of a functional mind-set . . . as well as out-and-out ignorance as to the social and political perspectives:

▶ **"She's so narrow-minded that she rejects all my attempts to help her!"** Surely the problem is *her*. It can't *possibly* be that your approach makes your "help" seem like a threat, could it? After all, you're Mr. Smooth, right?

From the functional perspective, trying to figure out what people want to hear and then repackaging the way you frame things is completely unnecessary and a waste of energy. Other people know what you mean—or should!—without having to be told. After all, you're transparent, right? I mean, really. Modifying your approach is political snakery, pure and simple. Why, that would be like . . . like . . . using a line to get someone's attention at a bar. Who does that?! I mean, when you're attracted to someone, you don't plan out how you're going to get that point across in a way that ensures receptiveness! You just walk up to the person, tell her or him exactly what's on your mind and what you want to do, and that's it! Works every time, right?

What do you mean, *not necessarily*?

Hmmfph.

How we say things has a big impact on how we're received.

▶ **"If everyone just did their jobs, none of these problems would exist!"** Yeah! That's right! If everyone just did their jobs, all our problems would go away! We'd be like a colony of ants, with the power of their ferocious efficiency! And all we'd have to do then is figure out what our jobs would be! Which . . . I guess means we'd need someone whose job it was to figure out what jobs the rest of us should do . . . and how many of us there should be for each job. This person could also stick around and referee problems that come up from time to time when jobs overlap, or when market conditions change and render certain jobs unnecessary. Yeah, that sounds like a good idea!

I wonder what we should call that person's job?

Maybe—here's an idea, oh ye functional thinker, tell me what you think of this one—we can call that person's job *management*.

▶ **"He's a moron."** You may be right about that. Score one for the functional perspective.

▶ **"My boss refuses to give me the tools I need to do my job."** When you say *tools*, are you talking about things like—oh, I dunno—the space to go figure things out for yourself? The challenge to create your own work environment? The ability to define your own job based on your own unique skills and abilities, as opposed to some contrived job description that was written before anyone knew how special you are? By *tools* do you mean your boss refuses to micromanage you and tell you exactly what to do, and when, and how, down to the last nitty-gritty detail?

▶ **"I do all the work, and he wants all the credit!"** Yes, the credit! I gotta get mine before you get yours, right? It's a dog-eat-dog world, and I gotta look out for number one. It's all about the Me, baby. I'm the corporate ninja around here, and I deserve my props! You should *see* the stuff I've done. I've got *credit*, baby!

OK, let's come back to Earth here.

Credit? You want *credit?* What are you trying to do, earn some kind of street cred with your cube mates? Are you in some sort of cubicle gang or something, where you get a tattoo of a staple on your arm every time a project of yours is successful? Or is it that you're trying to polish up a résumé that wouldn't be necessary if you focused on creating more Magic Moments at work? We spend so much time today talking about personal branding and getting credit for this and that that we often take our eyes off what's really important: doing good work. When you do good work, you achieve results, which strengthens both your résumé and, more important, your reference list.

I don't know about you, but I'm thinking that if (results + references) > credit, and (results + references) = good work, then by the transitive property: good work > credit.

The reason these statements are so easily twisted is because they work only on one level—the functional level—of the three you'll find in a typical career path. All I need to do is to assume the perspective of the social or political level, and I can turn these statements into dog meat and make anyone who's ever uttered them look silly. No offense. I know you're not silly.

Understand the Three Perspectives

The three perspectives work like this. When you first start out in your career, you do a job. At this point, success requires you to perform as a *functional expert.* That is, you need to be competent in your work. That is all functional expertise is: competence. Early on, your jobs will feel like extensions of the classroom, with set rules of engagement, limited flexibility, and clear authority, so the same abilities that got you through school will also get you through here.

Until one day you do your job so well that you get promoted into some form of management position. Suddenly people don't just want you to do the work anymore, they want you to engage others to do the work. They may even want you to delegate your functional responsibilities altogether.

"What am I supposed to do now?" you ask. "Whenever I use my functional abilities now, my team calls me a micromanager, and my boss just shakes her head in frustration!"

The answer is to become more of a *social expert.* As a manager, your job is to build teams, maintain teams, settle disputes among team members, negotiate with clients and vendors, get people promoted (including yourself, team members, and key outsiders who are friendly to the needs of your team), fight for resources, convince and sell, close the deals that others can't . . . basically, your job becomes to interact with others. It's the sandbox all grown up—instead of trading Snickers bars and arguing about who's going to play with whom, you trade business deals and argue whether to keep the team you've got or to reorganize.

Until it happens again: you've done your job so well that one day you get promoted to some form of executive position. Now even your social skills are not enough. No matter how good your solution is, and no matter how good of a guy you are, if you are one of four VPs and there is only one president's position, the four of you will no longer be friends. Especially if you're all young, in which case the three of you who don't get the job face the unpleasant prospect of possibly uprooting your families to accommodate your professional ambitions, or maybe putting a lid on your ambitions to accommodate your family. Yuck.

Things get even worse at the board level, where the line between personal and professional disappears entirely. I don't mean to suggest a systematic ethics problem at the board level . . . not at all. I'm just saying that when you have a group of people who, as a group, get to make the rules, and when you factor in human frailties like our tendency to be blind to our own limitations, strange things happen.

At the executive and board levels, you need to be a *political expert* in order to survive. You no longer "get things done" at this level. Not on your own, anyway. Instead, you eliminate the social and political barriers that stop others from getting things done. You buffer your team from other people's personal agendas, giving them the space to operate.

Herein lies the secret to eliminating fear: if you can understand what each perspective brings to a situation, and can determine the correct mix of perspectives to use to come up with a solution, you can eliminate fear by training yourself to see and deal with the *whole* problem, which will ensure that you have some action to take, even if that action is ferreting out and plugging up a little pocket of ignorance with genuine knowledge.

An Example of the Three Levels at Work

How many people do you think would say it is a good idea, when given unclear directions from a boss, to ask for clarity?

Probably a lot of people, I'd guess. I bet they wouldn't even give the notion a second thought.

But add some specifics and watch what happens.

Let's make these direction-seekers M.B.A. grads—very bright, well educated, and ambitious, like Jane Allayes from the introduction. Now let's fast-forward a few years after graduation. Our direction-seekers manage teams of their own, and they are all now recruiting newly minted M.B.A.s from their alma maters.

One afternoon, one of these managers—let's call her Amy—is interrupted when a recent hire—a person with the same intelligence, ambition, and solid educational background as Amy had just a few years back—walks into her office. This individual, on this particular day, desires clarity. "Amy," he asks, "The report you asked me to complete by Friday? I have some quick questions I'm hoping you can clear up for me. First, marketing has some information that we could use in this report, and I didn't know if I should go and get that information from them, or if you want me to build this report exclusively from intra-departmental sources. Second, how did you want this formatted? Will you be using this with clients, or is this an internal document? I don't want to burn too many hours on formatting if I don't need to. Third, when did you want this? I know you said Friday, but did you mean Friday morning or by the end of the day? Can I get it to you late on Friday? I have plans Thursday night. And finally, how will we be measuring my success on this project? As you know, I am interested in moving to the next level, and I'd like to understand how this project will help me get there."

Put yourself in Amy's figurative shoes. How does this conversation feel to you as a manager? From a functional perspective, it's all good stuff—"This is the project I was asked to do; now help me do it." But socially it's awkward, and politically it's a train wreck. Amy had hired a smart, ambitious M.B.A. on the hopes that this person would show the commitment, personal responsibility, and maturity to work through issues like this on his own, yet this new hire exhibits no personal responsibility, no commitment to the team, no indication of loyalty, passion, initiative . . . at some point, Amy starts thinking to herself, *What are they teaching in grad school these days? This kid's a mess!*

Rewind: you and Amy are the newly minted M.B.A.s with the questions about the projects you've been assigned. Is it still a good idea to walk into your bosses' offices to ask for clarity?

The upshot? You can complain that your company treats you like a cog in the machine all you want, but if every time you hit a roadblock you race to your manager and demand clarification, exemption, or redress, then you are sending a very real signal that you'd prefer to just limit yourself to the responsibilities enumerated on that bland, lifeless job description of yours. You are signaling that you want to be a cog in the machine. A job doer.

Is that what you want? To be a twenty-first-century brain laborer? To be employable only until an outsourcer—domestic or foreign, take your pick—comes in and shows how he or she can do the work less expensively? Or until someone writes a macro that renders your work unnecessary?

The functional perspective will not help you achieve career resilience. It will help you do great work, but great work alone is not enough. To ensure staying power, great work must be coupled with interpersonal astuteness and political savvy; the functional perspective must be matched with more social and political awareness.

Magic Moment Recap

Before moving on, let's bring back the Magic Moment concept.

Magic Moments are moments of deep, personal contentment. No matter what area of life they occur in, they can be created by the cultivation of three elements: commitment to objectives that are tough, real, and feedbacking; personal responsibility for environments that are conducive to the attainment of the goal; and a mind-set that is focused, persistent in that focus, and open.

Give that paragraph one more read-through. It'll help to have the Magic Moment model in your mind as you read the following chapters on achieving excellence within the three perspectives.

Onward!

WHAT YOU LEARNED

- ▶ **What is the top skill necessary to achieve Magic Moments at work and succeed in your career?** *The ability to shift perspectives—to understand issues from the functional, social, and political perspectives.*
- ▶ **What are the three phases of career development?** *Job competence (functional expert), management (social expert), and executive (political expert).*
- ▶ **What is an example of an activity that when viewed from the first perspective seems like a good idea but when viewed from a higher-level perspective can be seen as harmful to career development?** *Asking for clarity. From a functional perspective, this is a natural way to ensure good work. From a political perspective, this can signal a need for structure and an inability or unwillingness to solve problems proactively.*

6

Functional Excellence: Overused, Yet Never Enough

Functional Problems Can Be Solved
with More / Better / Faster / Smarter / Harder

Functional problems are often the easiest to see, but they are rarely root causes. If you spent your whole life trying to solve all the functional problems in the world, you'd never make a dent. In fact, if you had the power to freeze time and solve all of the functional problems in the world in the next instant, two instants from now the world would invent a whole new batch of functional problems to replace the ones you just solved.

This is because human beings are driven by emotion. As such, our functional problems are driven by our social and political perspectives. And while my definition of political has nothing to do with the liberal / conservative tripe peddled in Washington, geopolitics does give great examples of how political perspective shapes functional issues. Take the American Revolution, for instance.

The colonists—merchants, workers, and others—were having difficulty providing for their families. Their functional problem was that they were being taxed exorbitantly without any say in how those taxes were being applied by the British government. To the British government, the functional problem was that the colonists were not resourceful enough in their use of the natural resources they had at hand, nor appreciative of all they got from Britain. The Americans tried to solve their problem, the Brits tried to solve their problem, and ultimately a war was held to decide which side's version of events would be recorded by history.

If you could go back and freeze time so you could solve the functional problems of the day, what exactly would you do? A Brit might make American soil more fertile. An American might make Britain pass a bill authorizing an American member of parliament . . . or reject the Stamp Act. Ultimately, anything you do would have a minimal effect on the political struggle between the two sides. Solving the functional issues might delay some things, but unless you were able to get inside everyone's heads and literally change their perceptions of the world around them, all your functional changes ultimately would be for naught. As you removed the problems we know in hindsight to have prompted tensions between the two sides, different events would turn into triggers. So, did the Founding Fathers do all they could to avoid a schism with their homeland, or did they march headlong into a predetermined war? At a functional level, one could argue either side equally convincingly.

The lesson here is, if your goal in life is to be the world's best functional problem solver, you will likely remain at the mercy of forces that cannot be affected through your ability to do a great job. If you want a *career with staying power*, you need to create a mental model that goes beyond the functional level. You should understand issues as they appear to those with a social or political perspective; in other words, you need to understand your manager's—or even better, your CEO's—point of view. By understanding their social and political perspectives, you'll better understand the *why* behind your functional job description, giving you the clarity you need to work through, over, or around uncertainty in your job.

Without understanding these other perspectives, you have only a partial understanding of your issue. So when you try to solve it by working harder, it's like throwing darts harder to hit a dartboard you can't entirely see. How hard you throw won't improve your likelihood of hitting the board . . . but it will make the consequences of any mistake you make more severe!

Worse, when you are challenged by others about your decision to throw harder, now there is the likelihood that you will try to shift the blame for the consequences in order to protect yourself from a lawsuit. (It's amazing what people will convince themselves of in order to maintain a self-image of I-wasn't-really-that-dumb-was-I.)

Looking at the Functional Perspective from the Corner Office

Congratulations, I'm promoting you to CEO. Come with me to the door of your office—I want you to look out over the company. See all those people? They all work for you. Now let's take the elevator to the floor where the old you works in your old job . . . hey, there's your replacement! Say hi!

Now let's imagine your replacement asking you one of the very same questions the old you probably wanted to ask. Something like "Uh, when you say, 'process improvement,' what exactly do you mean?"

OK, fair question, but hang on, there's more. Before you answer, let's get your other three thousand employees all circled around you, too. They all have similar—but different—questions, and they're going to ask you their questions . . . now.

All right, *now* you can answer. And keep in mind, these thousands of questions are all very straightforward, and everyone expects you are going to respond immediately, because really, how long does it take to answer a simple question? Never mind that at one minute per answer, working straight through, it would take you more than two days to get back to everyone. No one thinks like that. They just want their answers. Immediately.

Oh, wait . . . here comes your assistant with a stack of messages . . . looks like you've got a few customers wanting to meet with you, a government official would like a word, you're being served a lawsuit by a disgruntled former employee who says she was discriminated against because her boss asked her to cover her belly button, there's a binder of sales numbers you need to look at before next week's board meeting, there are three other binders with information related to those acquisitions you asked your M&A team to look into, you have a request from a magazine for an interview for next month's feature article, and finally, there are three calls from your daughter from college and one from your son wanting to know if you're going to make it to his high school basketball game tonight.

And your employees are *waiting* . . .

Lovely.

Now rewind the clock. You're still CEO, but no one's asked you any questions yet. We're standing there, looking at your replacement, watching, and we have the power to imagine a different future.

Instead of three thousand people all asking basic questions, we can paint a different picture.

So, what picture do you want to paint? Here's an idea: what if your replacement—and his 2,999 colleagues—could figure things out for themselves? What if, given the chance to ask a question, what they said was, "Hey, thanks for the opportunity to work here. My manager helps me eliminate roadblocks, and while nothing is perfect, I can see good opportunities for me to grow into the next level. Do you think if I organized a lunch for my team and our clients, you could come for a few minutes to share whatever you can about our strategy?" What if you heard that three thousand times? What would you think? My guess is that you'd think, "Wow! How did I get so lucky with all these self-starters?" You'd also do the math and, assuming that each team had ten people and you would be speaking to entire teams, figure out that the number of times you'd need to answer questions would shrink from three thousand to three hundred and would include clients, too. Still a lot but certainly more manageable. Then, because you're a true leader and not a self-serving crook, you'd press forward in your efforts to build the world's greatest company, jazzed by what you just saw.

In this example, the difference between having an organization of people who need everything laid out in excruciatingly close detail and one in which people are able to take the essence of a direction, figure out what needs to be done from there, and get the job done is the difference between the CEO needing to engage three hundred times (with teams) and three thousand times (with individuals). To you, the CEO, that is an order of magnitude difference!

Chances are, you will be much more receptive to those who demonstrate an awareness of the challenges you face, and much less receptive to those who simply expect an answer and get aggravated when it takes a few days for you to respond. In fact, when they express aggravation, you may be inclined to tell their bosses to remove them from consideration for a promotion, because it's clear to you, from their behavior, that they do not appreciate—and therefore cannot possibly be prepared to handle—the attendant social and political pressures.

By the way, you're not CEO anymore. Sorry.

Master Functional Competence

Mastery of the functional perspective may be insufficient, but it is nonetheless a prerequisite for long-term success, and it starts with functional competence. At the functional level, competency means being able to make tactical, day-to-day decisions with confidence and accuracy.

These smaller, tactical decisions represent the smallest bits of uncertainty you are likely to find at work. If not dealt with the right way, this uncertainty can become pockets of ignorance and then fear. Therefore, your job from a functional perspective is to continually refine your models to strip away as much uncertainty as possible from the job. Think checklists, process maps, facts, and flowcharts.

To the functional mind, decisions are concrete and bounded: you may not know which direction to take, but you know where you are, you know where you want to go, you understand the decision before you, and—if you're competent—you either know how to make this decision or can construct a set of criteria for doing so on the fly. Both your issue and your solution set are limited in scope. Functional uncertainty is straightforward, like a fork in the road.

"Yeah, real straightforward. Except last time you focused on uncertainty, you told me I'm not allowed to ask for clarity. So what the heck will you have me do now, *guess* which option I should choose?"

Very funny. No, don't guess, use that prodigious brain of yours you're so proud of to fill in the blanks! When you got yourself hired—tell the truth now—did you tell the hiring manager you were a nitwit who would crumble without crystal-clear directions at every turn? Or did you try to impress upon her that you were a proactive, self-starting problem solver?

Has it ever occurred to you that a proactive, self-starting problem solver might not run and ask for help at the first sign of difficulty but might actually solve the problem on his or her own?

And before you say that you tried to solve the problem on your own first but couldn't, I'm going to tell you, that's donkey nuggets.

Tell me: before you hit the fork in the road, *when you didn't have any decisions to make*, precisely which *problem-solving* skills did you think you were using?

Following directions does not require problem-solving skills; it requires the ability to do as you're told. Correctly navigating a change in course, on the other hand, requires problem-solving skills. Reaching that fork in the road and having the wherewithal to make a decision—that's functional competence.

So when you hit a fork in the road—or any roadblock that forces you to choose a new direction—that's not the end of your ability to move forward but merely the start of when you need to engage your brain!

Ask the Right Questions

"What if I'm not smart enough? What if when I get to that decision point I freeze?"

Knock it off. It's not a question of intelligence; it's a question of temporary ignorance. At least for now. If you can ask the questions *why*, *what if*, and *then what*, then you're smart enough to beat ignorance. It may take you longer than it does for others, and you may need to go through some extra steps, but you'll get there. Business, as they say, ain't rocket science.

Make Time by Caring Less About Looks

To free up extra mental cycles for solving work-related roadblocks, eliminate the cycles you spend caring about pretense. Simply put, trade the effort you put into maintaining surface-level appearances for effort you can apply to developing true competence. Worry less about how you'll look when you build a new report no one's seen before and just build it. Take the time you were going to spend sending an uppity e-mail explaining the chain of command to an ambitious subordinate and instead spend it researching that acronym you heard at this morning's meeting.

Seriously, if you're still putting on airs after the crash of 2008, you really deserve a swift kick in the butt. Did you learn *nothing* when the market tanked? Go find work you *love*. Surround yourself with people you *love*. Find a place you *love*. Put yourself someplace where you can focus on doing good work, doing good deeds, making good things happen. We're done with title inflation and measuring each other by the size of our offices. Let the money come, and whatever it is, live within the means it provides and be thankful that you are surrounded on all sides with *love*. Put yourself in a position where you can be good at your job, and channel those ambitions of yours that you used to channel into gunning for the biggest title, fastest track to management, or shiniest car and put them into being the best at your work.

Have the courage not to care about pretense anymore.

Focus on More / Better / Faster / Smarter / Harder

If you are sharp and disciplined and enjoy your role as a functional expert, then, just by doing what you do, you will push the envelope and get ahead.

Bear in mind, many others will move faster than you, grasp more than you, be better than you, be more productive than you. You may be surrounded by people like this. Or maybe among your cohort, you're the fastest thinker. It doesn't matter. Do your best to remember your place in the bigger picture. Open doors for people who need your help, while learning from those who can open doors for you. Whatever your field, take the role of artist, scientist, or teacher: create new things, create new knowledge, or help make what exists more accessible to others. If you're not doing one of these three things, you're wasting everyone's time. If, when you engage functionally, you are doing one of these three things, then, on behalf of humanity, I thank you.

Functional Competence Versus Intellectual Ability

Many people will claim to be looking for smart workers when what they're really looking for is awareness at those social and political levels. At the functional level, excellence is not about raw intelligence as much as it's about working hard to maximize your output, pure and simple. At the functional perspective, success is about knowing what to do with what you've got.

"What if my job demands a level of critical thinking that is beyond my intellectual limit?"

Then shrink your world until you are able to understand it. Get yourself onto a team of smart people who can help pick up the slack.

"Doesn't surrounding myself with people smarter than me put me at risk?"

What, are you mistreating your teammates and encouraging them to look for ways to sabotage you and steal your thunder?

Being honest about your abilities and surrounding yourself with intellectual horsepower doesn't put you at any kind of risk. Lying to maintain appearances puts you at risk. Surrounding yourself with overly ambitious, terminally cutthroat sociopaths puts you at risk. Solving problems? Not so much on the risk.

Choose wisely.

Use More / Better / Faster / Smarter / Harder to Create Magic Moments

Good option: ask yourself the following questions to keep yourself and your team in control of the functional elements of your work. Better option: ask these questions of the team to get on a path to more Magic Moments for all members.

MAGIC MOMENT CHECKLIST

- ☐ Do you have the right goal—and is it clear? Can everyone involved articulate what it is your team is trying to accomplish, and why?
- ☐ Are team members committed to the team's goal and their individual goals within it? Beyond their paychecks, do members have a reason to care about success?
- ☐ Are your milestones realistic? Milestones can be tough and challenging, but is there consistent agreement about *how* tough they are? For instance, does the amount of time you have to accomplish a task reflect what your team can do, given its level of proficiency?
- ☐ Look across the team—what feedback are team members getting from and giving to one another? This isn't just your Magic Moment but theirs, too. Are the status updates, meetings, town halls, phone calls, e-mails, and texts getting the right information into the right hands? And what about the "white" space—the unofficial, informal communications? Are your team members' conversations on Facebook and Twitter reinforcing the team objective or corroding it?
- ☐ Are the people on the team in the right positions given their skills? If your answer is, "Yeah, I think each of us can do our jobs," then the next question to ask yourself is, "How do I know that?" Can you write out your answer in a way that would be compelling to someone else? Or would a guy like me look at it and push back on you that your reasons are more wishful thinking than actual reasoning? What about you yourself—what job are you being asked to do, and can you do it? If not, what do you need in order to become capable?
- ☐ Physically, is everyone in the right place? How is space affecting your team? If you are geographically dispersed, how are you using technology to bridge gaps? If you work in close proximity to others, how does that proximity help you or hurt you—do you have

members who have to spend time dealing with nosy neighbors? Do you have a gossip in your midst with access to enough information to create problems? Do you have a gossip on the outside who, unless provided with enough information, creates problems?

☐ Do you have the right resources? Assuming the timeframe is fixed and given only the tools you have, what is reasonable to expect in terms of the quality of your deliverable? Does this match with the expectations implied by your goal?

☐ Do team members take personal responsibility for getting things done? What happens when a problem pops up—do people step up and say, "I'm on it," or do they send ambiguous, unhelpful e-mails to all that say, "Someone should own this"? Do people communicate proactively? Or do they wait for others to come to them? Which behaviors are you modeling for your peers?

☐ Are you focused on your work? Or are you distracted by appointments on your calendar, non-project-related work, and/or personal investments? And don't you dare tell me you're doing everything possible to make the project work while simultaneously looking for a new job! Your brain is never off; what you do after hours directly affects your on-the-job performance . . . as anyone who's ever plodded through work with a hangover, or grumped about all day after a fight with a significant other the night before, can attest. The impact is not always so obvious as when holding back a wave of alcohol-induced nausea, but suffice it to say, putting energy into a job search, even if you yourself don't feel it, will limit your ability to focus at work.

☐ Is your team persistent? Or do people get discouraged easily?

☐ Is the team open and patient? Are you enjoying the process? Are you comfortable knowing that the outcome of your work will be determined later, but in the meantime, you're going to enjoy every minute of where you are—ups, downs, and all?

In the Magic Moment model, it is often the case that if one area is out of whack, the other eight areas seem out of whack, too, and when one thing clicks, everything clicks—even if only for a Moment. If your team reaches a point when making changes no longer yields lasting benefits, that's a clue that you're no longer dealing with a functional problem and need to shift your perspective to a social or political level.

For instance, in Bruce Tuckman's model of team dynamics from 1965—which Patrick Lencioni did a wonderful job converting into an actionable tool in his *The Five Dysfunctions of a Team*—the first thing a team has to do is to come together, or form. If a team moves too quickly through this intial phase, relationships don't gel and trust isn't sufficiently established between members to solidify a sense of team. This is a social level issue, visible from the social perspective but not necessarily from the functional perspective. To a functional thinker, the team's problems may seem to include people not showing up to meetings, not taking each other seriously, or not communicating with one another. People don't know why the group exists, what's expected of them, or what to expect of others. Instead, each member appears to have his or her own one-on-one relationship with the leader, and that's it. Functional thinking might lead to the team drafting project plans, proposing a team mission, or enumerating roles and responsibilities. Ultimately, none of these documents will stick, because the issue is not caused by a lack of documentation; it's caused by a lack of viable relationships. That's not to suggest that a team should not try to solve these functional issues. It needs to remain cognizant that when functional solutions fail to solve the problem, that is itself an indication that the problem exists on a different plane.

You Are an Environmental Variable in Your Own Magic Moment

Look at yourself as a single environmental factor for a moment, and ask yourself: do you have the technical / industry / mechanical knowledge to do the job?

If you look at yourself and say, "I cannot do my current job without additional support," then you should look to solve your problem at a functional level, by taking a course, going back to school, getting a certification, or asking your boss to walk you through an example.

If you look at yourself and say, "I can do this job," and then add, "but it's still not getting done. I wonder if I got an additional degree, or rotated through that other department, or took another course, if that would help," then you need to hit the pause button. Because as useful, fun, and valuable as those things might be, none of them will solve your problem. If you can do the job but are still having issues, then it's not your functional abilities holding you back but your social or political ones.

When More / Better / Faster / Smarter / Harder Is No Longer Enough

At some point, no matter how much you focus on the elements of the Magic Moment, you may find you cannot create them. When that happens, step back. You've been solving the wrong problems and need to change course. But before you do that, you need to understand why, when you discover that you need to change course, you are really, really not going to want to.

Functional Perspective Addiction

Since preschool, you have been trained to use your functional perspective above all else. Whatever the problems you were solving in class, the way you solved them used a functional approach: bounded, with a known range of variables, a known range of solution sets, and a known range of potential outcomes.

Then here comes the real world.

In the real world, a functional perspective will help you excel *in a job.* Hanging onto it too long, however, will keep you blind to what's happening around you at the social and political levels, creating pockets of ignorance and allowing fear to stymie you in your career progression. This is what happened to an attorney I did some work with a few years back. We'll call him Timmy. Timmy's story illustrates the risks inherent in using a functional perspective to solve a social problem.

The partners at Timmy's law firm were clients of mine. We'd meet regularly and discuss a range of issues related to the firm's operations. These were good people—human and imperfect, sure, but good. We spent a fair amount of time early in the project discussing the culture of the firm. One of the ideas discussed during these sessions was that law firms can be divided, loosely, into two types. To understand Timmy's derailment, it's important to understand what these two types are.

The first type of law firm is compliance-oriented. The guiding philosophy these firms hold is that they are risk mitigators. They focus on knowing the law and keeping their clients firmly within the boundaries of what's safe. They focus primarily on avoiding conflict.

The second type is guided by a more advocate-oriented philosophy. These firms believe that their job is to take the side their client during conflict by finding a friendly interpretation of the law. They assume that laws written with the best intentions sometimes fail to account for various specifics, and by serving their clients' interests, in court if necessary, they force the legal institution to clarify its intentions for the current case and for all of posterity.

The cultures of these two types of firms are quite distinct, and both are necessary for a smooth-running judiciary. Not every person or corporation seeking legal representation has the same risk tolerance or wants the same thing; some want to understand all the potential interpretations of a given law so they can operate in an area of common understanding. Others believe more strenuously in a particular interpretation and may be willing to risk being told no for the chance to shape the law. Timmy's firm was run with the philosophy that a law firm should advocate for its clients.

Neither philosophy is right or wrong. If we had only literalists, then we would have no case law, and every question of interpretation, no matter how trivial, would have to be settled by Congress through new legislation. Nations that use that system are eventually known as dictatorships. (As an aside, and as an example of why a functional perspective is insufficient when solving problems, political partisans will often complain about judges who "legislate from the bench" with regard to laws they don't like. When they complain, they often leave out the fact that creating case law, the real term for what's going on, has its roots in the Magna Carta and provides the public with an additional check on legislators' power beyond the ballot box. Gee, now why would they leave that out? Though legislators use a functional perspective to paint a black-and-white case of "judges should focus on their job, not ours," a political perspective reveals that by narrowing the judiciary's power, they expand their own.) On the other hand, if we had only interpreters, then no case would ever be settled out of court, everything would go to trial, and even more disagreements would result in legal battle.

A year into our project, one of the partners pulls me aside on our way out of a morning session. He tells me Timmy's work product is fantastic but his attitude is bad, and he's making choices that lead to unnecessary workflow challenges and put coworkers in a tough spot. This partner likes Timmy and sees a career for him "if he can pull himself together."

Would I talk to Timmy?

Of course. I went and talked to Timmy.

The answer to my opening statement, which was, to the best of my recollection, "Hi, Timmy," was a barrage of unsupported complaints with no structural theme. Timmy took advantage of my presence to launch into a diatribe about others' work ethics, the hours he was being asked to work, his lack of administrative support, and a host of other things that he could not, objectively, support with data. I sat down. I listened, took notes, told him that with his permission I'd look into things and that I would follow up shortly.

I'll cut to the chase: addressing issues related to workflow did not make Timmy's problems go away. All those functional-level, I-can't-work-smart-enough / fast-enough / well-enough issues he liked to complain about were red herrings. Timmy's real issue, as it turned out, was that he was uncomfortable interpreting the law. He was a bad fit for the culture of the firm. I quickly discovered that nearly everyone saw this except Timmy; Timmy's insistence on approaching his work functionally created a pocket of ignorance in his mind that swallowed up all the cultural and philosophical issues at play and blinded him to the social and political ramifications of his work.

The only issues Timmy could see were the functional manifestations of the deeper issues. What he saw was the jumbled mess he barfed at me during our first meeting; he did not understand why he was being asked to do the things he was asked to do, he did not understand why partners had reorganized his team, and he did not understand why one of the partners seemed to have stopped listening to him. He saw no theme or pattern because the pattern, which was rooted in the culture of the firm, existed at a social perspective that Timmy refused to acknowledge.

The partners understood that Timmy felt uncomfortable pushing the limits to create case law, and they were OK with that. Maybe the comfort would come with time and experience. Maybe with maturity. Maybe never. It didn't matter; they thought Timmy did good work, and they knew plenty of cases would benefit from his risk-averse perspective. They wanted to keep him around and reorganized a portion of the firm to feed Timmy a steady stream of work they knew he would be comfortable with. But when Timmy was given that work, he didn't see any of that reasoning. He saw only his functional reality, which was that he was being removed from the main flow of work through the firm. Trying to interpret his world solely from a function perspective, his version of events went as follows:

► **Timmy expresses concerns about case; partner disagrees.**
► **Pattern repeats with other cases until partner's behavior becomes dismissive; Timmy concludes the partner's actions are based on a lack of respect for the law.** This is the point at which fear begins to form in those pockets of ignorance. Timmy does not recognize the social perspective being used by others, and in the darkness he starts throwing those

darts harder. In this case, that means hardening his perspective with judgment. He fills the vacuums in his awareness with an interpretation of those around him that allows him to hang onto his original interpretation more tightly. He does not accept responsibility for the problem.

▶ **Timmy is told he will no longer be working on the type of cases the firm specializes in. In Timmy's mind, a red flag goes up: I am being silenced by someone who doesn't like me.** Timmy still does not recognize that to the rest of the firm he comes across as immature, nitpicky, and risk-averse to a fault. He is not thinking about social relationships. He is thinking only about the cases. His fears grow, and as they do his interpretations of what's happening in those pockets of ignorance become more elaborate. Timmy never questions his own perspective or professional maturity, only the motives of others.

▶ **Timmy's questions start him wondering about the ethics of the partner trying to silence him.**

▶ **Timmy starts to revise his interpretation of history.** Of course! The partner is unethical! That's why he didn't listen to me in the first place! That's why he silenced me by reorganizing my department so I wouldn't see those files! He's up to no good because he knows I was getting too close to finding out his secrets!

▶ **Timmy raises the issue with others, including paralegals, ostensibly trying to ferret out information and enlist support but really looking for validation for his assumptions.** When validation doesn't come, Timmy faces a choice: he can say, "Hmmm . . . other people whom I respect disagree with my perspective, maybe I'm wrong," or he can say, "Uh oh, the partner has already 'infected' my friends with that unethical worldview of his." The former option requires him to move into his pockets of ignorance with this new knowledge and possibly admit he was wrong; the latter he can do while ignoring contradictory feedback. Since Timmy has already labeled the other side as unethical, admitting he was wrong feels incredibly risky. He presses his case within the firm even harder, rationalizing to himself that he is the sole voice of reason at the firm.

▶ **Management approaches Timmy to help him out. Timmy thinks he must be getting super close to a nerve if management is paying him this much attention.** He's right, but he's got the wrong nerve in mind.

Timmy's fears cost him dearly. He failed to correctly interpret his environment's feedback, missing several opportunities to pull back from his mistaken judgments, in turn aggravating coworkers and showcasing his professional immaturity. Timmy, who could have enjoyed a long career at this firm, or at least could have left with the understanding and support of his coworkers, ended up quitting rather abruptly, leaving the firm on bad terms and walking away from dozens of quality relationships.

Without a social perspective to help him understand, Timmy could not accurately read the patterns in the world around him and marched off a cliff, from a career perspective. How come? Why did he cling so tenaciously to his functional perspective, even after it started getting him into trouble?

Timmy's functional perspective may not have helped him see the right story, but it did help him see a story, and a consistent and plausible one, at that. At no time did Timmy think he was the one who didn't understand what was going on. Timmy, like many others in a similar position, approached his work world like a school problem, connecting the dots as best he could and expecting to be treated like a star student when he presented his manager with his observations. When his boss didn't say, "Very good, Timmy, excellent point," but instead said, "That's not the way we do things around here, Timmy," Timmy had a functional way of explaining that, too. After all, Timmy had experienced bad teachers and bad administrators!

So while this was the moment at which Timmy should have elevated his perspective, there was no way for Timmy to know that. His perspective never stopped feeding him actionable information. What Timmy should have been paying attention to—his level of frustration, inability to create team Magic Moments, diminishing trust in coworkers—all require a social perspective to be seen. It's a bit of a catch-22: functional thinkers, until they accept the possibility of non-evil social and political perspectives, find themselves returning to a functional perspective in force just at the moment when they should be abandoning it.

WHAT YOU LEARNED

► **How do I know if I am dealing with a functional problem?** *Problems that can be solved with more / better / faster / smarter / harder tend to be functional problems.*

► **What is the key to functional excellence?** *The competence to make tactical decisions with accuracy and confidence.*

► **What is the danger of surrounding myself with people smarter than me?** *None. The problem is in surrounding yourself with overly ambitious people, or in mistreating those around you.*

► **How do I know if what I thought was a functional issue is social or political?** *When working more / better / faster / smarter / harder no longer solves your problems!*

► **What is the risk of staying too functionally oriented at work?** *While others address issues at social and political levels, you see only the manifestations of their actions. This can lead to misunderstandings and, if you are not careful, erroneous judgments about the people you work with.*

Social Excellence— Now We're Getting Somewhere

Learn to Interpret

Timmy is not the only person to make the mistake discussed in the previous chapter. Remember Jane from the introduction? The fast-track wunderkind who flamed out as CEO?

In the real story, Jane never made it to CEO. She had the same problem as Timmy and got brushed aside at the VP level as a result. (I am disappointed to report that Jane, while representative, is not allegorical.)

She blamed it, not too subtly, on the glass ceiling, but to those around her it was clear that discrimination was not the problem. The problem was that she never moved beyond her functional mind-set. She failed to respond to the copious amount of indirect feedback she got as an executive. In fact, she failed to even recognize the feedback she got *was* feedback. When people gave her half-smiles, lukewarm appraisals of her work, or belated invitations to critical events, she failed to interpret their behaviors, instead making literal reads: *that person smiled; he said he liked my work; I got invited.*

Her inability to interpret anything but the most pointed, actionable feedback, her repeated requests for clear direction, and her insistence that *all* behaviors and outcomes be subject to formal metrics all signaled to the incumbent CEO, the board of directors, and her peers that she could not handle the ambiguity she'd encounter in the CEO role. They wondered aloud how she could create direction for others when she had trouble creating direction for herself.

When this concern was posed to her, Jane balked, saying the executives were playing games with her by not giving her the direction she needed to grow into the CEO role. She countered that her job today was not the same as what her job would be as CEO, and therefore her success and preparedness should be based on her ability to perform the functions she had today. Besides, she was very good at creating direction for herself; she did it every day. To which they replied, "Jane, you're performing wonderfully in your current role, and everyone would be quite pleased if you decided to stay in that position for years and years and years. But you've asked to be considered for CEO, and that's a different ball of wax." They disagreed with her assessment of how to gauge preparedness, saying, in effect, Jane the Rule Follower was unlikely to magically become Jane the Rule Maker the morning she signed a new employment contract. They also outlined how her version of "creating direction for herself" still presupposed the support structure provided to her by her boss—how would she do when the support structure was removed? When she had to operate solely on the indirect clues such as the ones she had difficulty reading? They needed her to demonstrate CEO-caliber thinking *now* in order to give them the confidence that she could hit the ground running. They needed her to prove *now* that she could go beyond her functional perspective and approach her job from social and political perspectives as well, since much of the work she would face as CEO would be at those levels. They needed to see that she used every mental construct in her arsenal to eliminate her pockets of ignorance, and they needed to see that now, not because it was required in her current role but because it would be required in the role she wanted.

If you owned the company, wouldn't you want a CEO who could hit the ground running? If you were going to take a risk on someone, wouldn't you at least want a person who demonstrated a willingness to get in front of the learning curve rather than someone who tried to argue away your concerns? Wouldn't Jane's responses create just the sort of interpersonal friction between you and her that you'd be looking for her to remove from the organization?

Jane got frustrated and ultimately left. Maybe she was afraid of making a mistake. Maybe she was afraid of being trusted with that much control. Maybe she was afraid of facing the feedback she knew she was going to get. She had always been at the top of her class based on external metrics such as grade point average; in the business world, similar metrics had governed her performance. I think using those external metrics had allowed Jane to avoid acknowledging some things about herself she wasn't such a fan of—including her need for structure—and she was afraid of what she might find when she was put to the test. What if she were merely average? What if she didn't measure up and got kicked out? What if she were replaced by someone she had stepped on during her climb up?! What if what she learned about herself caused her to rethink her personal life as well as her professional one . . . would she have to acknowledge to herself that she was to blame for her last, painful breakup—that all the invectives she had hurled at her ex were really just projections of emotions meant for herself? Ouch!

Never underestimate the lengths people will go to in order to avoid having to admit being wrong. The ego is a powerful force. And one of the things the ego likes about the functional perspective is that seeing yourself as great functionally requires no self-awareness.

Broaden Your Focus

Jane couldn't make the transition. She couldn't even see it. All she knew how to do was to tweak and tweak her functional abilities, given the structure and constraints she was used to. When others asked Jane to think more broadly, she would go back and redo her financial forecasts . . . or apply a different strategic model . . . or make some other adjustment to the functional aspects of her work . . . but she never challenged her perspective; she never moved the walls she had put around her work. She never dove into the assumptions that underpinned her financial models and wondered where those assumptions came from, or whether she could unilaterally affect them.

Like Timmy, whatever Jane did came from the perspective of working more / better / faster / smarter / harder. When those above her said, "Hey, Jane, it's not about the work anymore; it's about you and your relationships," she either couldn't or wouldn't process the request, and her career stalled as a result. Many people get stuck like this. They manage projects to the letter of the contract, dismissing client concerns because they are unaware that there could be an alternative interpretation of what was written. They complain about being unable to engage socially because of stringent RFP processes, unaware that they can make a good impression even if the only opportunity they have to do so is during a two-second handshake. They argue that doing business with people you like, rather than people who are good, is unethical, unaware that it's quite natural for friendships to grow out of successful business relationships and vice versa.

As Jane's and Timmy's stories highlight, and as these experiences reaffirm, broadening your focus requires more than engaging in new behaviors. It requires expanding your field of vision, eliminating your pockets of ignorance, and moving into a role where you are an orchestrator of Magic Moments for yourself and others, a shift that brings a fundamentally different perspective about the world and that reinforces a sense of personal responsibility.

The Social Perspective: Solving Your Problems with a Handshake

Social issues can't be solved with more / better / faster / smarter / harder.

When you first enter the workforce, you are generally hired to do a job—to be a functional expert. As you move up, your jobs become more complex, until one day you get that promotion into a management role. Now you are expected to exist beyond the functional realm. You are told to rely on your people to do the work. What is expected of you at this stage is that you hire a strong team, support team members, negotiate for resources, close the deals your team cannot, develop team members, discipline underperformance, promote stars . . . in essence, solve the people problems as opposed to the workflow problems. And these problems cannot be solved at a functional level. In fact, there is a very famous story that makes just this point—the story of the Tower of Babel.

In short, the people on Earth, united in location and language, decided to build a huge tower that would reach the heavens. God didn't think too highly of the idea, so He foiled their plans. He didn't stymie people by taking away the raw materials or technology needed to build the tower, though, nor did he send down an angel to smite all the architects. What He did was, He made it so people spoke different languages, and He separated them physically. He created social-level barriers to their ability to build that tower that proved incredibly (perhaps a bit too) effective.

A group of people with the right social perspective can come together to accomplish any task. If they lack the functional skills to execute, they can obtain those functional skills. But a group of people with the right functional skills will never come together if they don't also possess the requisite social skills. For this reason, the social perspective is more powerful than the functional perspective, and critical to any careerist looking to achieve staying power. My experience working with people is that most of us, if we think about it, can find a time in our career when we were held back when we overemphasized a functional approach and missed something critical at the social level. Following is the story that stands out for me.

I had a boss once who didn't like me. At all. He was my lead for a client project, and while walking through the halls of the client organization one day, we happened to run into the CEO. The CEO wore jeans and went by his first name, so I greeted him casually and asked him if he would share a minute with us to discuss a project we were working on. My project leader was a far more formal individual than I, with a much different idea of how to treat those with formal authority. He read a lot into my actions: he thought I was disrespectful to the CEO, for one thing. He thought I was disrespectful to him, for another. And he thought my engaging the CEO showed a(n obvious) willingness to circumvent the proper chain of command, which in his mind raised all sorts of questions about insubordination, proper training, and ethics. Me, I was just taking advantage of a chance encounter with a leader who had demonstrated a relatively low regard for formal authority to get a quick answer to a pressing question. Imagine my surprise when my boss accidentally e-mailed me a draft of my upcoming performance review, and I saw the boxes labeled "needs improvement" checked in every category, and comments in areas that were supposed to be descriptions of my work that read, "Jason is the most arrogant individual on the team . . ."

I was stunned.

Let me assure you, no amount of more / better / faster / smarter / harder was going to solve any of these problems. I had committed the cardinal sin of not following my boss's lead in terms of how we were going to get our work done. I had violated our team's implied social contract about how to accomplish our goals, and I nearly got creamed for it. My reaction was to want to call my boss out for clearly not understanding the purpose of a performance review, for not telling me about the problem while I still had a chance to fix it, for not more clearly setting expectations for me as a member of his team, and, most of all, for being inept with e-mail. I didn't. I simply forwarded the e-mail on to my boss's boss, who was the intended recipient. When the issue on the table requires a social solution as opposed to a functional one, don't argue, don't fight, don't complain. The problem needs to be solved at the level where it exists, and complaining lies exclusively within the domain of functional thinking. Even if you're not sure what you should do, *don't do that!*

In this example, what stood between me and a Magic Moment wasn't functional; it wasn't the *what*. My boss and I had exactly the same goals, on a macro level, at least. I was delivering objectively good work already—a lot of good that was doing! What differed between us was *how* we wanted those goals achieved. For each of us, the *how* was implicitly baked into the *what* in ways we couldn't see.

We both wanted to achieve our shared goal the most effective, efficient way possible, but what did this mean? I looked at the situation and thought, *Our client is a fast-moving, growing organization and is looking to our team first and foremost to show them how to get things done. My job therefore is to see where politics are holding them back and demonstrate to others how to dismantle those vapor walls.* My boss looked at the situation differently. Based on what he saw, he would say, *Our client is a fast-moving, growing organization and is looking to our team first and foremost to model a disciplined approach. My job therefore is to do things the right way as best I can and then raise the issue when I hit a roadblock.* In his mind, we were surrogate employees, hired to do a specific job and responsible only for ourselves as environmental variables. In my mind, we were strategic partners, brought in for our expertise and expected to share it with others.

Because of our different perspectives, and especially because in our dynamic it was the junior consultant pushing for the more strategic interpretation of our role on the project, we were destined for a problem. No amount of focusing on the work was going to solve it. This was a social problem through and through, entirely based on our shared (mis)understanding of the situation. We had taken the time to discuss *what* we wanted to do, but not *how*.

And that was my fault.

One hundred percent mine.

This is important: if you're thinking, *No, your manager shares some responsibility for the mess because he didn't align the team's expectations, and clearly he didn't communicate his expectations to you, as evidenced by the fact you were surprised at the draft review*, then you're thinking like a functional expert. You're looking at job descriptions and roles and responsibilities and trying to figure out who was supposed to be doing what, and when. But remember, our problem wasn't functional in nature. A functional discussion might have highlighted differences in our perspectives, but only insofar as they affected our actual work. Had we discussed and planned and clarified functional roles and responsibilities ad nauseum, it would not have stopped me from reaching out to the CEO when we caught him walking down the hall. Even had my boss and I agreed to approach our work as hired hands, it would not have stopped me from reaching out. I would have handled the conversation differently, but in my brain I would have thought, *Hey, there's the CEO, I bet he might like to know what's going on at the ground floor. Plus, maybe I can get information about what other needs the client has we might be able to fill, which my boss would like to know for when our contract is up.* I still would have said hello and engaged him. The problem between my boss and me had to do with our social philosophies, not with our roles and responsibilities.

I had the power to solve our social problem. Had I gotten to know my boss better, had I paid closer attention, and had I let go of *my* judgments of *him*, I would have perceived his comfort zone and seen how I could have kept myself within the parameters with which he was comfortable. That's not a roles and responsibilities thing, that's a human interaction thing. And since I had the ability to drive that change, since I was 100 percent capable of getting the information I needed to avoid the problem, I must therefore claim to be 100 percent responsible for the problem itself. Not because of my formal role, not because of my place in the chain of command, but because I had the power to anticipate and solve this social issue from the start.

Make Sure Your Goals Are Mutually Agreed Upon

Sure, you can set a goal for yourself, but as we can see from Timmy's, Jane's, and my own experiences, setting goals for yourself may not always be the best idea. If you are operating at the functional level, setting a goal in a vacuum leaves you exposed to risks you don't anticipate. To generate staying power in your career, *you* need to be in control. Functional goal setting is what you do when you want a job where your only concern is meeting the expectations of others. For careerists, this will not be enough; serious careerists do not put their fate in the hands of others.

You cannot approach goal setting, therefore, as a solitary endeavor. You may think you're operating alone, but at some point, my guess is that you'll want someone to notice what you're doing . . . and not just any someone, but someone looking for a person with your talents and willing to pay more for those talents than you are making right now. How much easier your career will flow if your goal and that other someone's goal have been aligned ahead of time!

It's Actually Not About You

The bigger reason not to go off and create goals in isolation is that no one really cares about your goals. They care about *their* goals. They care about your goals when doing so helps them with their own.

This isn't cold-hearted, this isn't bad, and this isn't an indictment of mankind. We all need to take care of ourselves. That's not evil; that's responsible. There are six billion people on this blue marble of ours; if you subordinated yourself to them, you'd quickly find yourself exploited. And if they stopped caring about their own goals, they'd find themselves exploited, too. So, to some extent, to each his own. But also to some extent, "to each his neighbor's": to succeed in this networked world of ours, part of our goal-setting process needs to include helping others achieve their own goals, because we need their help, and one way to earn their help is to help them.

Best of all, the process of setting mutually acceptable goals yields important clues about how other people want to work and be treated. Beyond the specific goals, you can tell by the process how the individual approaches his or her world. Had I done this with my project lead, I would have seen his formal style, and had I reserved judgment, I would have been able to successfully adapt to it.

Helping One Another Is More than a Mutually Beneficial Transaction

Helping one another is more than the transaction visible through a functional lens. There are social and political aspects to helping one another as well. For one thing, deals are not always bilateral, nor fair in an economic sense. I might help you and ask that you repay me by helping a third party. Or I may ask you for nothing in return for my help, and you may (or may not) respond by paying the help forward. Moreover, helping people has an emotional component with real value that cannot be accounted for at the functional, transactional level. Pretending otherwise is like trying to value the role of a stay-at-home parent according to the various different jobs the person does (cook, valet, chauffer, etc.).

The ruse doesn't work. It may make for some thought-provoking conversation about what salary you'd ascribe to the job of raising children ($134,121, according to Salary.com), but push enough and the whole thing falls apart. Emotional benefits exist on a different plane from the functional work being done, and those cannot be economically valued. We cannot yet put a price on love.

That's the truly beautiful thing about Magic Moments: there is an element to them that goes beyond a functional transaction. Yes, the more you help others achieve theirs, the more they'll help you achieve yours, but there is more to it than that. We may not have the scientific know-how to measure it, but we feel it and we know it's real. When we stop looking for that emotional connection and focus solely on the transaction, we've *sold out*, or worse. At work, when all you get for your efforts is a paycheck—that is, when your commitment to your job hinges exclusively on the functional arrangement—you're called a clock puncher. You're *mentally checked out, a drone, unfulfilled.* And management? They're *money-hungry, soulless slave drivers.* It's not a pretty picture. Whatever you do, when operating socially, you'll push to give and get more from the arrangement than a few bucks; you'll help set up one another's Magic Moments.

One day science will catch up and we will be able to measure things like friendship, love, and trust . . . but until then, we should neither pretend the answers can all be found in our roles and responsibilities nor confuse the immeasurable with the unimportant.

Make the Shift from Functional to Social

Many people, while working as functional practitioners, adopt a fighting mentality that makes the future shift into a more socially oriented role particularly difficult. Some of these people have conditioned themselves to distrust, under all circumstances, anyone who doesn't have a craft or who wears the title of manager (especially if they do so with pride). These folks speak about management with obvious pejorative overtones. They commiserate about offenses real and imagined, and when they need an enemy, they name it management. How does someone from this group become a manager? Not easily.

This person has built a fence around his functional perspective; crowning him manager will not instantly give him visibility over that fence. He is bound to carry his pockets of ignorance with him into the new role, because presumptions, judgments, and attitudes are hard to let go of. As a result, he is also bound to struggle as he continues to favor the celebrated, but insufficient, functional perspective and continues to demonize the social perspective he needs to be successful. He can't just switch sides. Every time he considers approaching things socially, he is going to fear losing his old friends, being called a hypocrite, or selling his soul. This is Timmy.

Of course, he created this reality for himself, but that's cold comfort. As they say, you reap what you sow. The sooner you stop judging, the easier you make your eventual transition. Even if you want to remain in the position you have, letting go of judgment will help you build the relationship you need with your manager to negotiate viable goals and be successful in the long run.

Some people are not judgmental about management, just uneducated. They simply never give any thought to anything beyond the functional work they do, so when they get tapped for a more social role, they lack the fundamental understanding of what the role requires. I frequently see salespeople, engineers, and service professionals such as consultants, attorneys, and accountants who fit into this category. Jane fits into this category. These are people so ingrained in their jobs that they struggle to let go of functional responsibilities when placed in a management role—either they ignore their managerial responsibilities or they go too far the other way, becoming a caricature of the overly formal, hierarchical archetype manager.

Know When to Let Go of Your Functional Perspective

Getting this transition right is as important as any management certification or degree you might be thinking about going after.

As difficult as the transition can be, it is nonetheless important that careerists get it right. The results of overestimating the importance of a functional mind-set can be pretty ugly. Just ask Jane what she thinks of her career stalling out!

The challenge is that there is no bright line you cross when it's time to shift to a new perspective, no roadside marker to let you know it's time now to think more socially and less functionally. You never open your door one day to find your sienna-tinted functional farm replaced by the Technicolor plants of a more socially oriented Munchkinland. Reality is far more subtle.

It's not the kind of thing you can "try harder" at, either. Trying harder implies doing more of the same, and if you're doing more / better / faster / smarter / harder, then whatever you're doing, you're reinforcing your functional perspective, which is the very thing you need to *let go* of. Letting go allows nature (which hates a vacuum) to fill the void with something else. You keep trying out these something elses that nature is bringing to you, and you keep discarding them, until you find the something else that fits. Something more . . . social.

And what could keep you from letting go? From cycling through various different approaches? Oh, I dunno . . . maybe ignorance, arrogance, judgment . . . *fear.*

When you are afraid, you tense up, close ranks, and hold on tight. You shut out the world. Fight or flight, baby! Watch others around you. When they are afraid of not measuring up, they'll reject opportunities to advance (flight), or start changing the metrics so they can prove they're better than others (fight). (And really, who among us hasn't done both of these things on occasion?) Once that fight-or-flight instinct gets triggered, you have an issue—namely, you're no long working in the realm of conscious thought. You're operating based on instinct, and the conscious brain is woefully underpowered given the task of harnessing raw emotion.

Look what happened with Timmy. He kept closing ranks until he convinced himself there was something unethical going on, and once he did that, there was no going back. That level of judgment tripped a wire that made him afraid to the point where he could no longer think rationally about his situation. Jane, too—the more she fought, the more tenaciously she clung to her views, the more judgmental she became until she also reached a point where she could no longer comfortably agree to disagree; she had to leave. In both cases, the objective reality never changed. Had Timmy filed an ethics violation complaint, or had Jane filed a discrimination lawsuit, so what? Even if they had prevailed, given their circumstances, all they would have accomplished would have been to establish legal rationalizations for their mistakes and create unnecessary wreckage. They would be no closer to success, either today or in the future.

You cannot push. When you are afraid, your brain freezes. Forcing the issue reinforces this process, making letting go an even more difficult proposition than it was to begin with.

Learn Active, Continual Adaptation

One way to move past the conundrum of needing to relax right at the moment your feelings of fear flare up is to adjust your mental model from one of periodic change to one of continual adaptation. When you find yourself needing to adapt to something, whether it's a new situation or other people, the mental construct you hold includes three phases: your current phase, your desired phase, and the transition phase between the two. This model presents a number of challenges in world of rapid change:

1. Two out of the three phases—the transition phase and the desired phase—represent unknowns, and unknowns are scary. The model is twice as scary as it is safe!
2. When you view change as a discrete thing that happens periodically, even if your brain knows the change is necessary, it will devote thought to the idea that it can be avoided or postponed.
3. The world sometimes moves too fast: you may not have a chance to move halfway through the transition phase before something new happens and your plan becomes obsolete, causing you to have to switch gears. How exhausting!

By contrast, active and continual adaptation means accepting change as the norm. Active adaptation means releasing any expectation of the future whatsoever. Active adaptation breaks the assumption many of us live with that tomorrow will most likely look like today.

(Have we not learned recently that all is not as it seems in the world? That major institutions can crumble overnight? That new technologies can become global phenomena within a matter of years, months, weeks?)

What worked in the past worked in the past; what works now can be expected only to work now; what will work in the future will be something we have yet to experience. By giving up the assumption that what works today will probably work tomorrow, we can react to changes more quickly and more effectively. We don't waste money trying to protect a temporary present; we don't waste energy wondering what might be; we don't waste time waiting for the future to happen. Active adaptation means proactively moving into the future every moment, constantly testing and refining methodologies as we go. With active adaptation, we live *in* the now and live *for* the future.

When you actively adapt to your environment, many functional-level struggles go away. You no longer complain about "old-timers who don't get it that my cell phone is my lifeline," nor do you complain about "kids who don't have enough common sense to silence their phones while at work." You no longer see change as the crashing of two solid forces; change becomes more fluid, more continuous— softer in some ways, more powerful in others. With active adaptation, there are only two things in your world: there is what you do to create a Magic Moment, and there is the feedback you get that lets you know if you are successful.

That's it. Just you and a sea of feedback, letting you know how you're doing. A surfer navigating wave after wave of life experience. Mahalo, my friend. Welcome to the world of active adaptation.

Find the Balancing Point

Consider this: if it's in your world and you didn't create it, then it's feedback.

Now, me being me, the first thing I did when I thought about everything in the world I didn't create being feedback was to label the idea ridiculous and try to disprove it. If I turn on the TV and see a story about a flood halfway around the world, that's supposedly feedback I'm doing something wrong? That's crazy talk, isn't it?

Actually, it isn't. I have the ability to turn off the TV, no? If nothing else, seeing that story about the flood presents me with a choice: I can either help, or not. If I can't help, I just took my attention away from my sphere of influence and diminished my ability to affect my world by instead spending time on something beyond my ability to help. If I can help, great. Somewhere between these two extremes is a balancing point, at which I engage with mass media enough to benefit from an awareness of what's around me but not so much that I distract myself from areas I can affect. And if Nielsen Media Research is to be believed that in 2007 the average adult male really did watch four hours, thirty-five minutes worth of TV every day, then I think it's safe to assume that we're aware of the flood, we're not helping, and we're not focusing on our sphere of influence, either.

If I'm watching the flood, then, the feedback isn't that I caused this flood to happen; it's that I'm filling my days with negative stories that I can't do anything about. Maybe I should turn off the tube, huh?

That story on TV is no different than someone calling me up and telling me about his bad day. Sometimes I'm in a position to help. Sometimes I'm not. And sometimes the person doesn't want help; he just wants to complain. It's up to me to control who I listen to on the phone and in person; similarly, it's up to me to control what I expose myself to on TV.

The truly wonderful thing about active adaptation is that, by reducing the world to goals and feedback, it puts you on a path to use your time more wisely.

Use Active Adaptation to Hone Your Goals

Active adaptation puts us in control over our own destiny. I've said it before, I'll say it again: that can be frightening. When you start to take

control, you lose the ability to point your finger at others in blame
. . . *you're* in control, and that means *you* are responsible—good, bad,
or otherwise.

There is another side effect to taking control of your goals through
the process of active adaptation: blind hatred, blind ambition, even
blind faith all get obliterated. To be sure, hatred, ambition, and faith
themselves continue to exist—they must! These are human qualities
with a rightful place in a complex and beautiful society, providing
balance to love, humility, and reason. What changes is that they are
no longer *blind*. Active adaptation to our environment encourages
conscious choice.

Following is what the active adaptation process looks like when
applied to the Magic Moment goal-setting framework.

Create a Draft Goal

Start with a goal. Any goal, go ahead, pick one. Even better—*remember* a goal of yours.

If you're struggling to think of a goal, put this book down and
go for a run. Or a drive. Or a walk. Relax, unwind. You have a goal
somewhere in your mind—busy yourself doing something mindless,
and it will come back to you.

And for heaven's sake, when it does come back, *write it down* this
time!

Seek Feedback

There are two types of feedback: direct and indirect. You will not
always be in a position to ask for direct feedback, and sometimes,
when you are, the person giving the feedback won't have the awareness, courage, or words to give you what you need. In these cases,
you'll need to look for indirect feedback.

In software development, direct feedback would be a beta user
sending in an e-mail with a screen shot of the failed application, along
with a description of what she was doing at the app's time of death.
Indirect feedback would be information available from crunching

usage statistics to see how many times a button was clicked in a particular type of application usage.

In the real world, direct feedback is someone sitting down with you and telling you, "When you come to work wearing four-inch platform shoes, tank tops, and neon orange headbands, Howard, it makes me feel like you don't take our medical practice's dress standards seriously." Indirect feedback is listening for whether someone responds to you with an automatic "Yes!" or an ". . . uh, yeah, sure," and trying to determine if the pause was pregnant with unspoken disappointment.

Many people fail to correctly spot and interpret indirect feedback. They either don't know how to read their surroundings or they fail to account for the impact of their emotions.

I got a phone call from a friend of mine about a year ago. He was telling me about a salary negotiation he was having with his boss when he said, "So I was upset and probably a little emotional when I told him I didn't like his offer, but still, his response was totally out of line!" I asked him to tell me exactly what he said, and when he did, I laughed. Couldn't help it. Sometimes, when it's not being boring, the truth is better than fiction.

"You said that, and you think you get to absolve yourself of your role as instigator?"

"But he should've known I'd be upset. He had it coming!"

"Whaddya mean, 'he should've known'?! If someone on your team said what you had said, you'd fire him on the spot, and you'd be justified for doing it!"

My buddy guessed I was right, and he patched things up with his boss. Refusing to acknowledge your impact on others is a favorite tactic of self-destructors and the single best way to ensure you miss all the glorious indirect feedback the world is sending your way. In my friend's case, the feedback he was getting was twofold: the salary negotiation told him his value economically and his not getting fired told him something about the trust he had built up with his employer.

When you establish your goal and start soliciting feedback, make sure you interpret the feedback the right way. If you have a trusted friend, parent, mentor, or coach, this is the time to use that person. Ask him or her to call B.S. on you. And if you don't have anyone, visit me at http://jasonseiden.com. You're not alone, and your problem is not insurmountable. Whether through coaching or a connection, I'll get you the help you need.

Get the *Why* Behind the Feedback

Directly or indirectly, find out the *why*. If possible, have this conversation away from the original piece of feedback. For instance, if you get a surly "good morning" from a woman who's normally quite effervescent, you can say something like, "Hey, you don't seem quite your bubbly self this morning . . . did I catch you in a bad moment or maybe do something I wasn't aware of? Can I help put the bounce back in your step?" This approach, executed with genuine empathy, is disarming. It strips the ego out of the conversation, allowing the person to tell you if you messed up without hurting your feelings, and communicates your desire to help. This moves her closer to her own Magic Moment—in this case either closure with you about something you did or perhaps closure on an unrelated issue with which you can help—and also builds the relationship so that she's more willing to help you with your Magic Moment later. It's all good. And if you don't have the presence of mind to do this in the moment, you can approach her later in the day and have the exact same conversation.

If you don't genuinely want to hear what she has to say, however, don't ask. Try this approach without empathy, and you'll come across as a disingenuous sleazeball. Sometimes, despite the best of intentions, you may still appear sleazy; genuine is in the eye of the beholder. You'll know instantly if your sincerity is in doubt if she rolls her eyes at you; that's not her being rude, that's her telling you *you have not earned my trust*. When this happens, you don't need to dig any further; you have located the source of the feedback—you are perceived as untrustworthy. That's what you have been looking for. Go with it. Don't worry about what she actually says or doesn't say; it doesn't matter. The heart of the problem in this case is a lack of trust.

Build Trust

When you discover someone does not trust you, that there's a game ender, stop the questions; your new, interim goal and the next step along the path to your Magic Moment becomes: build that trust. (Or walk away and figure out how to achieve your goal without this person.) Don't waste a moment being disappointed or angry; it doesn't matter. Genuine is in the eye of the beholder. (Anyone else having déjà vu?) Let's turn the tables to understand why, once you pick up on a lack of trust, you need not push for any more information. Say you don't trust me. When I come to you for information, what are you going to do? Despite what you might tell yourself right now as you think about it, I can tell you what you'll do, because I see it constantly: you are going to filter, whitewash, slant, and otherwise polish everything you tell me. There is nothing I can do with any of what you tell me—none of it's any good. You're telling me a story. You don't trust me with the truth.

Well, if my whole modus operandi is to take full responsibility for my goals, to eliminate fear by closing the little ignorance gaps in my awareness, certainly using whitewashed information doesn't do me any good. I need real data and honest opinions. Otherwise I'm solving the wrong problems. And by the way, I can't force you to trust me. At least, I don't think I can.

Or can I?

Let's play this out. If you roll your eyes at me, and my reaction is to call you rude, and tell you how open and honest I'm being, and berate you for meeting my genuine attempts to engage you with snotty, sophomoric behavior, would that win you over?

No? OK, I was right—I can't force it.

When there is no trust, the feedback is that *there is no trust.* Then it's up to you to decide if the lack of trust is due to an environmental variable that is within your ability to modify, or if the lack of trust is due to irreconcilable worldviews that make it better for the two of you to just go your separate ways.

(How can I be so sure about this? Because I've been watching this dynamic for nearly a decade. When a consultant, after a two-hour interview or a half-day of training, starts telling you things about yourself that you barely admit to your spouse, your defenses go up. You want to know how this consultant knows so much and who else he's been talking to. One of the pieces of feedback I get is that what separates me as a management consultant from my peers is that I not only get the assessment right but I am also able to navigate past people's defenses and earn their trust, too. Do I win over everyone? Wouldn't that be nice? Still, several thousand people later, this is a pattern of behavior I understand pretty well.)

Use That Information to Negotiate the Goal

Armed with solid feedback, go back and modify your goal! Not the core element of what you want to achieve, but, at the margins, make adjustments to close the gap between impossible and merely tough; negotiate the *how* so you are in a position to help people achieve their Magic Moments and they are in a place where they want to help you with yours. Create interim goals where necessary to build relationships and to get access to resources that will be important later.

Negotiate the Goal, but Don't Compromise

When I say negotiate, the word that flashes in my mind is *trade-off.* Treat goal setting as an iterative process that, like software development, has beta and production releases but no terminal end—there is always something else that can be thrown in later. This approach allows you to constantly focus on a concrete, stated goal while also refining a future iteration. You can do this through trade-offs, where you exchange discrete items of various value. What you can't do is iterate through compromise. Once you've shown your willingness to split the baby, so to speak, you're toast. You've devalued your goal, and you can't get that value back.

When people say "never compromise," what they mean is, never *compromise*. That doesn't mean make yourself inflexible. Avoid "splitting the baby" or settling for less than you're worth. You are well within your rights, however, to make trade-offs in order to get through impasses. In fact, you should negotiate. Your goal does you no good if no one buys into it.

These are the steps to approaching goal setting from a social perspective: seek feedback, build trust if necessary, and use what you learn to negotiate a mutually acceptable goal without compromising your core interests.

Concentrate on the *How* in Addition to the *What*

Functional excellence is very *what*-centric. Social excellence is not. Social excellence is all about the *how* . . . and the key to the *how* is in communication.

How you say what you say colors the meaning of what you say. (You may need to read that a few times to follow it.)

People who believe you can convey "just the facts" are conveying both the facts *and also* a message that they wish to remain functionally oriented. They are limiting themselves by making it so that only audiences whose filters are similar to their own can understand them. Don't buy it? Stand in front of a mirror with your arms held out wide, like you are about to give your reflection a hug. Smile at how ridiculous you look and say, "Get your butt over here."

How playfully charming.

Now fold your arms, furrow your brow, snarl, and say the same thing, "Get your butt over here." Seems to have lost its charm all of a sudden, huh?

Five Elements of Communicating "More Perfectly"

Want to succeed? Want to negotiate goals that will set you up for Magic Moments, more easily control your environment, and help yourself and others maintain winning attitudes? Yes? Then you need to communicate "more perfectly." You need to take full responsibility for all of your communication.

One hundred percent, full responsibility.

This means that you own every miscommunication you have. If someone misunderstands you, it is because you were not clear in your communication. If it turns out you misunderstood someone else, it's because you did not do a good enough job as a listener.

There are no other options.

This plan is exceedingly tough, frustrating (you won't win over everyone, even after you take full responsibility for trying), and, ultimately, incredibly rewarding.

It's also how you begin to shift from being a purely functional expert to someone who also understands the social perspective.

Tone

For many people, when they think about managing their communication, they think of managing their tone. Unfortunately, this thinking is often limited to voice inflection and body language, which are functional-perspective solutions.

Managing the tone of a conversation functionally means memorizing a complex list of poses and what each one means, as well as a range of facial expressions and how to contort yourself such that you're subliminally sending messages through your body language to reinforce the content of your message . . . and, of course, don't forget to do the cross-cultural analysis to know how to modify your behavior based on the cultural norms of the people you are speaking to. Alternatively, you can approach the subject from a social perspective, in which case you can focus on three things that, if managed even marginally well, will help make your behavior well received, regardless of how well you do at the functional level.

Catharsis = Problems. Whether you are talking on the phone, sending an e-mail, or looking someone eye to eye, if you are blowing off steam, you are not solving the problem. A catharsis is an emotional release. That may be important to help you move forward, but when you aim that release at another person, you very well may be just dumping your emotion onto that individual. Which means now *that* person needs a catharsis. Nice job. Unless she has nerves of steel and incredible self-control, she's going to find her catharsis by shifting all that baggage you dumped on her right back where it belongs, which is at your feet. Back and forth you'll go.

You can tell you are in a communication in which you and another are volleying emotional barbs and releases when, partway through, you realize, *Hey, we agree on the issue . . . why are we still fighting?* Right. It's because the fight doesn't end when the functional issue gets solved; it concludes when the emotional issue—the stuff on the social plane—gets cleared. Despite your agreement on the issue, the two of you are destined to trade your emotional turd ball back and forth until someone gets wise, walks away, or throws a punch.

Next time, leave the voicemail for *yourself.* Write the letter and e-mail it *to yourself.* Better yet, open up a word processor instead of e-mail, write the letter, and hit *save* rather than *send.* Then pop on the headphones, crank up whatever it is you listen to when you need something loud and angry, and hit the gym.

Assuming Flexibility Based on Power = Problems. One of my clients calls me to his office one day, and when I get there, he starts telling me how aggravated he is at me for ruining his life. I don't know what to say.

He tells me he had been perfectly content blaming everyone else for misunderstanding him, but since our conversation when I had told him that as CEO he needed to be "more perfect" than the others in his office, he discovered just how much work goes into being a good communicator. He tells me he realized he had been using his elevated position to excuse himself for communication gaffes—as both a talker and a listener—while also demanding more from those under him. "No one would give me a straight answer, and now I know why—I was a dictator!"

When he switched that around, he said, he started seeing better results—turnover went down, employee engagement metrics went up, productivity went up—but the price was steep. He could no longer shut his brain off.

"Plus, now I know what *real* frustration looks like; I see the problems I can't fix, and I can't even chalk it up to a misunderstanding anymore. It's either me not communicating clearly or me not listening carefully. I don't always have time to fix the problem—sometimes you just have to say, 'That's a shame' and let things be—but . . . I feel like I owe it to everybody to keep trying, and it's tough."

"Yeah, that's tough." I answered, nodding.

"There's always something else to consider, isn't there?" he says, shaking his head.

"And not just at work, either. You really should be communicating more perfectly with your spouse, too."

The lesson here is that there is always something more *you* can do to improve things, beyond figuring out what the other person could do better. There is always an action *you* can take unilaterally in a communication to improve the relationship, or at least mitigate its negative impact. When you cut yourself slack, or assume that your power entitles you to more wiggle room, you're inviting problems.

Anything That Causes Anger, Resentment, Hurt, or Frustration in Others = Problems. This one should be obvious: a negative statement or action, purposefully aimed at another and intentionally designed to cause pain, will certainly cause at least as much trouble as catharsis . . . right?

Right.

If you think of nastygram e-mails, gossip, and other negative junk as a virulent form of catharsis, you wouldn't be far off.

Actively adapt your communications to minimize the damage you do to others.

If you do nothing other than eliminate catharsis, assumed flexibility, and anger-inducing language from your communication, you will go a long way to improving the tone of your communication . . . and you won't need to memorize the different meanings of resting your elbows on the table versus leaning on your forearms.

Direction

Will this message be best received as a top-down directive? As a bottom-up movement? As friendly advice from a peer? As a suggestion from a customer or vendor? As an innocent question from a friend?

When actively adapting communication, one of the things to consider is from what direction the recipient of a message should be approached. Sure, it's your idea, but that doesn't mean that if you state it, it will happen. In fact, in many cases, you may be a bad person to deliver an idea, especially if you're not trusted. Another way to introduce a lack of trust into communication is to pick the wrong relay; for instance, managers who use subordinates to bring messages to the whole team frequently create trust problems because of the way they choose to communicate messages. Teams may not want to hear top-down directions coming from peers. Questions spring up regardless of which perspective you use to interpret the situation: why was *that* peer chosen to deliver the message? Does she have the ear of the boss? Is she being fast-tracked? Does she have political clout? Is there something going on I should know about? Did she understand the message correctly? Is she relaying it faithfully? Is she lying? When a message is delivered from an unexpected direction, it can create problems.

Timing and Frequency

Timing is everything. You may have something very important to tell me, but if you catch me on an afternoon when I'm putting out multiple fires, I could be too distracted to hear it—you may be better off postponing. If I just spoke with your boss, I may not want to leave her office and come directly over to you to discuss a problem I'm having with your work—you might assume I was just talking to your boss about you, which may make you nervous that maybe whatever I'm talking to you about is a bigger deal than I'm letting on.

You may not always be able to choose ideal timing—indeed, allow me to be the first to tell you, "There's no such thing as good timing!" But by considering the sequence of your actions, you may avoid the most troublesome potential problems.

As for frequency, it has been noted by leaders, with some frustration, that messages must be delivered repeatedly before people start to internalize them. It has also been said to those who repeat themselves too often, "Leave me alone, ya nag!" Active adaptation in this case means monitoring how often others hear a particular message and ensuring that your communication appropriately amplifies it without harping.

Why not just assume that because you've said something once the message was received? Never mind the psychology of listening, look at this question from a practical standpoint—people forget things, lose e-mails, get busy, and . . . did I say people forget things?

Keep track of your messages, who's heard which, and repeat them often enough. If it's an important mantra, risk harping.

Channel

As a consultant, the aspect of communication I see most frequently overlooked is what channel to use. Should the conversation be held face-to-face? Over the phone? Handled with a few quick keystrokes? Done via handheld? Many of us give the answer some thought, but our actions are driven by default behaviors rather than more purposeful analysis. What a shame.

If you get called into your manager's office to discuss what she says is a minor issue, you'll dismiss the "minor issue" label and assume this is a major issue. Why? Because who calls you into her office for a minor issue when she could have just said something to you during one of your many daily hallway encounters?

Similarly, if you choose to have a series of face-to-face meetings with your team members to deliver a piece of bad news, and you talk to me last, I'm not going to believe you when you tell me how important I am to the team, because *you decided to talk to me last.* (This is a pretty potent form of indirect feedback. It may not be a problem you want to "solve," per se . . . just . . . understand the message you're sending and be purposeful with it!)

Always be sure to choose a channel befitting the significance of the communication.

Content

Perhaps you've heard Albert Mehrabian's statistic about how in emotionally charged communications, only 7 percent of the message's content is conveyed through what is actually said?

Now put that finding into a broader context, where conversations don't happen in isolation but are pregnant with all the previous conversations you have had, and with all the indirect messages being sent through the timing, tone, channel, and direction of the message. It is certainly possible for an emotional charge to be picked up in your communication through all this. In fact, let's hypothesize that you meant to imply no emotion, but the message's recipient is looking at the context of your communication and drawing some inference about it; we don't know what. Here you come, assuming your message is devoid of emotional charge, ready to focus on the content, which is 100 percent of a nonemotional communication. Your listener, meanwhile, is geared up for an emotionally charged dialogue; your content only answers 7 percent of her questions. She searches your face and focuses on your tone to pick up clues as to the other 93 percent of your message.

If you're trying to convey just the facts, you allow your listener to come to conclusions unaided; you are putting yourself at the mercy of her ability to work through all those inferences she made without any help from you. What are the odds she'll get it right? Better question: what are the odds that her conclusion will have some impact on you? Why leave your fate to that kind of chance? Why not go beyond the facts, address the emotional, social aspects of the interaction, and know for sure where everyone stands?

From Functional to Social: It's a Perspective Thing First, a Behavioral Thing Second

Serious careerists need to make an effort to move from a purely functional perspective to more of a social perspective as quickly as possible, because long-term success requires many high-quality relationships. It is important to note that I am not merely advocating behavioral changes; the shift in perspective is bigger than how you walk into a room or dress. Those things matter, but they will fall into place on their own when your perspective starts to click.

Ever watch someone with a natural technology mind-set figure out a new device he's never seen before? No one has to tell him how to turn the thing on or how to navigate the menus. He has a feel for it. And while he sometimes makes mistakes, the people around him forgive his errors because of how quickly he masters the device. People with a truly social perspective are like that with other people. That's why they don't have to stress so much about how to dress or what to say—they've developed a knack for building relationships that let them focus on what's important, so they naturally start making better decisions about how to behave. And if they make an occasional "mistake," it's usually a forgivable offense.

Shifting your perspective is about altering the way your mind processes information and what it pays attention to. It's about blowing out those pockets of ignorance in your mental map by going beyond the *what* to also focus on the *how*, starting with how you communicate with the people around you.

Engaging at a social-perspective level means taking responsibility for all of your interpersonal interactions, and that is no trivial matter! You have a lifetime's worth of history thinking about people and communications in certain ways that you'll have to overcome, and whatever challenges you may be having now, you also owe all your success to the approach you've taken thus far. It's not as if people with a functional perspective—those who, at work, transact with others rather than focus on relationships and who focus on managing communication behaviors rather than communication impacts—can't make friends or never take responsibility. After all, human beings are social creatures; it's in our blood. For these reasons, it can be difficult to see the need to change. The thing to keep in mind is that there is one specific benefit to shifting from a functional to a social perspective that makes the hard work worth it: those with a social perspective are more powerful than those with a purely functional perspective.

A group that comes together can learn the skills it needs to succeed. A group that cannot come together, on the other hand, cannot leverage individual members' skills. There is real power in having the social skills to bring a group together! As you develop your social perspective, ask yourself: are you bringing people together, or are you like a building engineer at the Tower of Babel, shouting in a language no one else understands?

A quick final note for those of you who do need a jump-start at the behavioral level: go to http://jasonseiden.com/interpersonal-skills-for-introverts for a video containing specific, behavioral tips on how to engage others. Following the steps outlined in this video will help you get a taste of social success and help you internalize, a little bit, why transitioning to a more socially oriented worldview is a good thing.

Then take a deep breath, because if you think the transition from functional to social is tough, just you *wait* to see what comes next!

| IN THIS SECTION |

▶ **How do I know if I am dealing with a social challenge?** *When more / better / faster / smarter / harder doesn't help anymore. Social issues are solved with a handshake.*

▶ **How do formal roles and responsibilities limit my ability to address social issues?** *They don't. Roles and responsibilities govern the functional aspect of human interaction in the* *workplace. Social issues exist on a different plane; as a result, you are 100 percent personally responsible for all work-related issues at the social level.*

▶ **What elements of my Magic Moment are affected by my social abilities?** *When you work with others, goals and resources must be negotiated. You require social skills to build relationships and engage others to help you with your Magic Moments—often by helping them with theirs first.*

▶ **What is active adaptation?** *Active adaptation is an alternate view of change that breaks the presumption that the future will most likely look like the present. As a result, change is no longer viewed in three discrete steps (current state, transition phase, desired state), but as an ongoing occurrence with no terminal endpoint.*

▶ **When soliciting feedback, can I accept feedback from everyone equally?** *No. Feedback from people who do not trust you is unusable; when people don't trust you, it means they don't trust you with the truth. No matter what they say, you cannot be certain about the veracity of their feedback to you. In a separate issue, people who lack self-awareness may also not provide the most meaningful data.*

▶ **What are the five elements of communicating "more perfectly"?** *(1) tone, (2) direction, (3) timing and frequency, (4) channel, and (5) content.*

Political Excellence: The Price of Self-Determination

The third perspective used in the work world is the political perspective. Maybe this idea excites you. Maybe it scares you. Or disappoints you. Maybe you feel nothing. I can't know, but I do find most of the people I work with have some kind of emotional reaction to the word *politics*, and it's usually negative.

Whatever our feelings about them, politics exist whether we choose to understand them or not, whether we like them or not, whether we engage in them or not. Just as the stars in the sky show up night after night, regardless of our knowledge of astrophysics, so too politics exist in our world, no matter what we think about them.

The Moral Imperative: Politics Can Never Be a Substitute for Good Work

I did not write this chapter to make you a game player—don't you dare try to substitute something else for good, quality work. No! This is about protecting good work *from* something else. It's about giving the good guys the tools to *win*. This is written for the ethical, hard-working, deserving careerist who wakes up every day and gives it his all. This is written for *you*. Herein are the tools you need to make sure you never lose ground to those who play games and try to keep you under their thumbs. This is about helping the good guys win.

Controlling the Frame

If the functional perspective is focused primarily on the *what*, and the social perspective is focused more on the *how*, then the political perspective . . . is an entirely different beast altogether.

Politics is the process of framing issues to get people to perceive them in a particular light. It's the stage as opposed to what's happening on it.

Politics shapes both the *what* and the *how* by providing *control over the frame*. A simple example careerists would be familiar with might be a development plan. You want a promotion. That's the functional *what*. You know your boss is big on self-development, so you decide to demonstrate your worthiness for the job by requesting a 360-survey—that is, a survey of your peers, subordinates, bosses, customers, and vendors about your skills and overall performance. That's the social *how*. Now you also want to control the frame, so you carefully select the people you want to solicit feedback from. That's the political *frame control*. The presumption here, by the way, is not that you stack the deck in your favor—that's the version of politics in which relationships are used to displace quality work. The presumption is rather that you pick individuals who put you in the best light . . . *whatever that means*. Maybe you stack the deck with customers; in addition to soliciting feedback, by reaching out to more customers than internal peers, you are signaling, *Hey, boss, check this out: I'm not only development-oriented, I'm also focused on the customers' needs.* Or maybe you pull in contacts from all over the organization in order to demonstrate your breadth of relationships. Or you pick people who you know are power players to demonstrate the strength of your network. Or something else. The point is, however you slice it, you are trying to signal something with your selections, and when you do that, you are fighting for control of the frame; you are politicking.

Mastering the Mind-Set

The Magic Moment has three components: goal, environment, and mind-set. The functional perspective gave us a piece of the environment and the core insides of the goal; the social perspective gave us the sense of personal responsibility needed to ensure our goal and our environment are well matched; the political perspective will give us mastery over our mind-set and tie everything together.

Game, set, match.

When you can control the frame, you not only master your own mind-set but influence others' as well. When you don't control the frame, you are not sure how others interpret your intentions, and your plans are therefore vulnerable to others' misinterpretations, influence, and meddling. Even if that meddling is well intended, by people who truly believe they are improving upon your solution, it's still med-dling, the impact of which is that you end up with a goal you are not totally committed to, an environment you cannot fully control, and a mind-set dictated by someone else. Your Magic Moments are, at this moment, dependent upon others, and that's not where we want them. We want you in control of you.

Understand the Cost of Engaging

Every four years, America puts up several candidates for president and makes them duke it out for votes. Imagine you are one of them. You have your slate of issues, and you are running for the most thank-less job in the world because you truly believe in what the power of the office will enable you to do. You promise to take the high road in the campaign . . . but doing so costs you dearly in the polls. Your main rival for the job, the incumbent, strong-arms the press to deny you coverage. And your background is twisted, with your greatest accom-plishments used against you. You watch your opponent's machine working on you and it makes you want to scream. They skewer you in political cartoons, lampoon you in editorials, and mock you on late-night TV. Still, in your heart of hearts you know you have the best solutions, and you are committed to winning that office and seeing your policies enacted. Your enemy's dirty tactics have steeled your nerve. You think about all the volunteers who have come out to help you, all the donors who put their checkbooks and reputations on the line to support you . . . and you *want to win that election.*

The question is, how badly do you want it?

This is not a rhetorical question.

You cannot win the campaign by taking the high road; that much is clear. So you have a choice: you can run an honorable campaign that will lose, or you can run a dirty campaign that will bring you victory. If you run an honorable campaign, you will lose—that is a certainty. When you lose, you will then watch the country spend four years under the leadership of a person who stands for the wrong things, who fights dirty, and who seeks power for the sake of power. Running that "honorable" campaign, therefore, is tantamount to abandoning your principles. Or you can get dirty and win. If you do this, you will have a chance to use the office for good, but it is uncertain you will be able to capitalize on that opportunity. For one thing, you will be compromised; your campaign tactics will cause others to cast doubt on your sincerity. For another thing, when you take office, you will have just concluded an experiment in which a dirty, amoral campaign proved more effective than a moral, upstanding one . . . do I need to explain the temptation baked into that takeaway lesson? Finally, consider this: in the moment you discover how much power there is in hanging up your moral code, you will also be conferred with more power than you have ever had before in your life.

So what's the choice, really? It's this—lose and subject yourself to the will of others, or fight to win and never again be able to discuss your moral code with certainty, even if, after your victory, you do the right thing.

It doesn't matter if the prize is the presidency of the United States, becoming CEO of a company, or being promoted to manager of a division. The process is the same, and the sacrifices are the same. Only the scale changes.

So I come back to my main question: how badly do you want it? How important is it to you to control your own destiny—is it worth your moral code? If you say it's not worth sacrificing your moral code—that it's better to subject yourself to the will of others than to fight dirty—then I have to ask what happens when—not if, but *when*—your new superiors impose a morality upon you that you don't agree with? (We know it's a *when* because they were willing to engage when you weren't; we know immediately that their code is different from yours. We also know they have power over you, so it's only a matter of time before a situation percolates up when they impose a solution . . . a solution framed by a code you don't agree with.) Is it OK to fight back then? And if it's OK then, why not preempt? If you wait, you could be committing many, many people to get hurt. If you fight now, preemptively, you are the only one who gets hurt.

Understand the Cost of Opting Out

Political engagement is not for everyone, and there will be no judgment if you decide you don't want to engage. But understand the consequences: you automatically give up control of your own destiny. If you want to win—if you want to call the shots and control your own career path—there is no other way. You either accept the conditions of the game, or you submit to someone else's rule, or you join a group and submit yourself to its collective will (though if you do that, you'll be right back to trying to figure out who controls the group, playing a political game on a smaller scale), or you throw your fate to the hands of Lady Luck and go about your business, waiting for someone else to take care of you. These are the options.

So really, it turns out, there is no way to avoid politics.

None.

If you choose to operate exclusively on a functional or social level, you will be at the mercy of those who are more politically oriented, because they can control the stage upon which you are operating. You can claim that you are "above those types of games," and that's fine. It's just not true. No one is above politics.

"Jase, I'm uncomfortable with your insinuations here. Good work should be its own reward."

Agreed. And it is. It just isn't enough to ensure long-term success in a world with more than two people in it.

"Well, I refuse to be a game player!"

Good, you should refuse to be a game player. What you *shouldn't* do is refuse to engage politically.

Just because someone is politically oriented does not automatically mean he is underhanded or that he does not do great work—that's fear-based prejudgment right there, and that type of thinking will ensure you never eliminate the last pockets of ignorance in your mind. Remember a few minutes ago, when you were running for president? Were you being underhanded? Or were you doing what you needed to do to make sure the best solution was adopted?

I do not advocate gamesmanship. I do, however, advocate fighting for control of the frame. The person who gains control of the frame will have the best chance to orchestrate things in his or her favor, and will succeed or fail on his or her own merits. To someone operating on a political plane, failures are due to miscalculations or poor execution as opposed to any external forces. The political player is in control of her own destiny.

People try their hands at politics all the time—they just don't admit it. And no wonder! Would you admit that you're engaged in a battle to frame the way someone else thinks? Do you want to admit you're in a fight for the way you yourself perceive the world? "Hey, watcha gonna do today?" "Well, first, I need to make sure my boss thinks this project I'm on is a winner, so I'm going do good work, and then I'm going to do some extra stuff that makes me look super-shiny good in her eyes. It's totally gonna catch my team by surprise; I can't wait. Then, there's this hottie I want to take out this weekend, so I'm going to orchestrate things so she finds out I drive a convertible, then guide the conversation to the point where I can ask if she'd like to go for a ride. I know exactly how I'll do it, too—she'll say yes, for sure. Later this afternoon, I'll try to convince Dave to stop showing up to our Thursday basketball games by making it sound like a bunch of people are injured and unlikely to show. If I feel like it, I might throw in a political conversation for good measure; I just came across some awesome stats about global warming that should really make a tree hugger bend in the breeze—if you know what I mean—and I was thinking it would be fun to try it out on Mark! How 'bout you?" Not likely. We have words to describe people who talk like that, none of them flattering.

You'd likely deny you were engaged in politics if you weren't very good at controlling the frame, because you wouldn't want people to see you trying and failing. You'd especially deny your political maneuvering if you were good at it, because you'd want the quality of your work to speak for itself and wouldn't want people diminishing your quality work simply because you supported the work from a political perspective. Under no circumstances does it make sense to admit that you engage in politics . . . yet under no circumstances does it make sense to not actually engage!

Politics Is a Perspective

"It still sounds a little evil."

Stop with the judgment already, will ya?

Politics is not evil, politics is a perspective. What you're likely afraid of is what you'll see when you use the political perspective. When you look through a political lens, everyone is naked. Not that they aren't wearing any clothes, but that all the duality of the human condition is on display. Everyone's strengths and shortcomings jump out at you. You see what people care about, what tempts them, and how far they'll go for the things and people they love. Seeing this way forces you to confront the truth that the human condition is imperfect, and the political perspective puts those imperfections on display, bright and shiny for everyone to see . . . and use against you.

For instance, if you're principled, I can shame you into submission. If you care about people, I can hurt you into submission. If you're honorable, all I have to do is play the game and I've got you. Sun Tzu wrote about this twenty-five hundred years ago, and it's as true today as it was when he wrote it.

You know the climax of the typical action movie, when all the foot soldiers have done their thing, when the absolute villain meets the absolute hero in one-on-one battle? That's the political arena. And you know how the bad guy always has an ace up his sleeve—an extra knife on him somewhere, or a hostage the hero didn't know about? That's politics: the villain fights as hard as he can *and* takes the extra step to protect his interests. But you know what's not politics? The Hollywood ending. In real life, that little knife more often makes the difference between victory and defeat than the purity of the hero. To win at the political level, you need to be good, yes, but you also need to anticipate the villain's game and play the same game right back. If you haven't seen *The Dark Knight*, it's worth watching to see this dynamic play out: both sides pack extra knives (literally, it turns out), and both sides score victories on account of their deviousness. Batman, in fact, grapples with the exact problem outlined in the presidential-election scenario: he must break his moral code to protect it, and the movie does a good job highlighting the true cost of winning.

In life, if you're going to play to win, it helps if you pack that extra knife, too. (Metaphorically speaking, of course.) Politics is a zero sum game often won by the player willing to get dirtiest. I'd like to add ". . . without crossing the ethical line," but I can't. At the political level, you often have the power to move the ethical line to suit your needs.

The good news is that politics not only places your human frailties on display, but it also puts your virtue on display, just as bright and huge as anything.

In fact, you know what cemented George Washington as a national hero? His virtue. Here was a man who, as general of the Continental Army, had the power to stage a coup after the Revolutionary War was won . . . and didn't. As president, he could have anointed himself king. (American citizens, having been subjects of Britain up until recently, certainly were used to the idea of a sovereign leader.) He didn't. He could have run for re-election forever . . . he didn't. Each time he was trusted with power—each time his career took him into the political realm and he *won*, he had the integrity to step back and reset the ethical line. A weaker man might not have made the same choices given such temptations. Yet make no mistake—he had enemies among his contemporaries who distrusted him and doubted his sincerity. When Washington "reluctantly" accepted command of the Continental Army, he was dressed in his uniform from the French and Indian War, leading to speculation whether a "reluctant" man would have dressed to impress. He engaged in the politics, controlled his destiny, got himself into the positions he needed to hold . . . and then proved his doubters wrong by laying down his sword when the job was over. Joseph Ellis has written a remarkable book titled

His Excellency: George Washington that provides not only a fascinating historical account but also a riveting narrative of the politics of the day.

Political warfare is a Faustian bargain. You put your soul in hock in order to save it, and you hope you have enough goodness left inside you to remember to reclaim it when you're done. History gives us many clear examples of what this bargain looks like. Keeping with the presidential theme, there's George Washington, who—before he became a national hero—was a treasonous rebel; Thomas Jefferson, author of the Declaration of Independence, who nonetheless remained loyal to his state of Virginia on the subject of slaves. There's Abraham Lincoln, savior of the Union, who suspended habeas corpus—a fundamental tenet of our rule of law—and allowed roughly 2 percent of the entire American population to die in battle; Franklin Delano Roosevelt, who helped defeat Nazism by galvanizing America against the Axis . . . by allowing the bombing of Pearl Harbor despite prior knowledge of the impending attack; and Harry Truman, who definitively ended World War II by dropping not one but two atomic bombs on Japan.

Understand that when we talk about duality, the good and the bad both run deep. Without politics, we'd never see the underbelly of human nature, true, but we'd also never see how good people can be, either.

Engage Politically

Do you have a knot in your stomach just thinking about this? You should. Human beings are imperfect, and it stands to reason that by taking full control over our destiny, our imperfections should be apparent. That's not an easy pill to swallow; at the functional and social levels, progress means improving and getting better. Suddenly, at the political level, it can feel like we're taking a step backward, embracing the very flaws we'd been working hard to overcome in the previous two perspectives. It's natural to feel a little uneasy, or to want to work out the paradox I've painted for you by proving to yourself that you're not engaged politically despite my assurances that you are, or to come up with an argument that would prove that you *can* walk away from politics and still retain control over your career.

Duality. Paradox. Relativism. Lack of closure. Sacrifice. Welcome to politics. No one said this was going to be easy.

The act of holding a political perspective without violating the moral imperative will, most likely, put a knot in your stomach. This isn't a knot like the kind you get when you're facing a steep learning curve and wondering if you'll get over it, either. It's bigger than that. This is the knot you get when you have to fire someone. Or when you step to the edge of that super-steep, super-tough ski run and realize it has iced over and you are in way over your head. Or when you know that telling the truth will cause innocent people to get hurt yet you have no choice. It's the knot that comes with the awareness that someone is about to get hurt through your own action.

It's basically the feeling of wanting to throw up. I'm sure you know it. It's what happens when courage and fear collide.

The alternatives to the knot are bravado, which most of us have beaten out of us by our mid-twenties, and fear. Bravado comes from not fully understanding the implications of your actions. Fear comes from breaking the moral imperative: when you forget to take your soul out of hock and begin to substitute political will for good work, you may start to fear reminders of the idealism you once held. You'll do your best to hide that truth from yourself, generally by playing political games to crush whoever is tormenting you, but if you fail to outrun that person—if the person you try to crush turns out to be as tenacious and stalwart as Jimmy Stewart's character in *Mr. Smith Goes to Washington*, then you'll *really* want to throw up.

Orchestrate Your Own Success

"Bringing the discussion home to the work front: what *exactly* does 'controlling the frame' mean to *me* and my *job*?"

Controlling the frame means orchestrating everything about your own success. Within the context of Magic Moments, it means focusing so hard, persisting so willfully, and demonstrating such openness and patience that not even your deepest personal feelings for others will stop your forward progress. In tactical terms, it means being purposeful in everything you do and sending clear signals that shape the way others interpret your functional and social behaviors. It means accepting that good work is not always recognized as such and that people will need your help to understand just how good your work is.

Again, at the risk of sounding like a broken record, I need to repeat: *do not be a game player.* Since this may sound a little weak in light of the preceding sections, let me also say this: the difference between a politician and a game player is that, while the politician's feelings won't stop him from succeeding, he still struggles with them. He recognizes and appreciates that those are real people he is interacting with, and as he goes about his business, he also looks for opportunities to help. He cheers for others even as he plays his hardest to win for himself. He also makes sure that everything he accomplishes, after the cost of the path required to get there is accounted for, still results in a net improvement for the world.

Control the Frame in a Group Setting

Broadcasting one message to a hundred people is not the same as ensuring one hundred people all hear the same message. If we're going to control the frame, we need to make sure the one hundred people all hear the same message.

When I was twenty-six, a coworker called me a chameleon, and not in a good way. My crime was changing the slant I gave to an intracompany presentation I was making to several different groups. I had emphasized one point while talking to our team and a different point when talking with senior management. My coworker, a programmer, was a bit taken aback, and he argued I was being sneaky. He said the presentation should not be doctored in any way—I should put the facts out there and let people come to their own conclusion. I said the teams all cared about different facts and would come away from a fixed presentation with very different conclusions. He said it didn't matter. I said it mattered a great deal, that the idea was to engage each audience in the same story, even if that meant using different hooks to engage them. He thought it better to lay things out and let the chips fall where they may.

That conversation has stayed with me. I have had the opportunity to watch scores of speakers, politicians, commercials, movies, and other storytellers in action since then, and I've reached a conclusion about our disagreement: we both made valid points, but mine were more powerful. His argument was not wrong; it was just made from a functional perspective. I was thinking politically. Specifically, what I was thinking was *I believe too strongly in our project to put our fate in anyone else's hands but our own.* Had I made the same presentation to each group, I would have lost control of the project. I would have tele-graphed a functional mind-set, and each manager with a stake in our project, sensing a void in the leadership I was bringing to the team, would have tried to step in to provide the missing social and political leadership. By altering my emphasis, I not only aligned others' under-standing of what we were doing, but I also signaled that I understood how to engage at a political level. There was no leadership void, and so we remained in control over our own destiny. I remember trying to articulate this idea to my friend at the time; I think what I said was something like, "Dude, stop being such a tech weenie."

The power of a brand, or the brilliance of a speaker or the appeal of a movie, is determined by its ability to put a single image in audi-ence members' heads. Yet we're all different, with different mental filters. We have different aspirations, different demographic back-grounds, different behavioral patterns, different attitudes about life.

So how does a good storyteller deliver a single message to all of us?

The same way I handled my presentation: by delivering *many versions* of the same message to us. A good brand puts out multiple versions of a single message, each tailored for a different group of cus-tomers. A good movie or book makes each of us experiencing it feel the same thing, often by exploring multiple facets of a single emotion so that everyone who has felt that emotion—however they experienced it—can relate. Storytellers put multiple versions of their messages out there until they can be sure that when their audience is done processing, they will be holding the same image in their heads. They do this by creating associations, using metaphors, sharing different characters' points of view, and focusing on commonly understood details.

The trick is to deliver different versions of the same story and not different messages. A good storyteller always comes back to the same central theme, creating a pattern for the audience to follow. A good politician does the same. In the last election, Barack Obama was the better politician on this score: whatever a voter's issue was—the environment, Washington gridlock, the economy, foreign affairs—his answer always came back to the same key themes of *hope* and *change*. Everything he said was a variation of one of these central themes, and in that way he controlled the frame better than his opponents in the election. He told us how to interpret him, told us what to focus on, provided us with a persistent image to refer back to, and patiently waited for his opponents to make the inevitable mistake. He also did something else: he didn't try to win over everyone. He figured out who he needed and went after those people with a vengeance. If he didn't need you, or if you demonstrated that you weren't going to buy into his message regardless of how many times you heard it, he ignored you, never mind if it hurt your feelings.

Resistance to Politics

"Maybe I don't get it . . . you keep talking about presidents, but me, I'm a manager at a company. I am still resistant to this whole idea."

Did you see the movie *Hoosiers*? Do you remember the scene in which Gene Hackman has his team measure the court dimensions in that big arena? If you don't, here's the synopsis: a small-town basketball team shows up at this huge complex to play for the state championship. They are overwhelmed by the size of the arena, as they are used to their small gym back home. Hackman has them measure the court to prove to them they're playing the same game; the number of spectators will be (much) greater, but the game is the same.

The same thing applies to you and the presidents. Same dynamics, different scale.

As for reasons why people choose to avoid politics, from the executive assessments I have done, as well as the coaching, training, and consulting, there are four biggies that tend to stand out to me: lack of conceptual awareness, lack of a mentor to show them how to engage ethically, overexposure to a society that vilifies the political process, and a functional perspective of morality and ethics.

Lack of Conceptual Awareness

Of the three perspectives, the political one is the most conceptual. This immediately creates some challenges for some people, since not everyone has the ability or interest to engage long at a conceptual level.

It also means that those looking for a direct, linear connection between their activities and the results they are likely to achieve from those activities may lose patience with politics. Unlike functional work, which—even at conceptual levels—tends to be pretty straightforward, political planning is often circuitous and fraught with risks and probabilities. Politics is like chess: you make moves today to achieve results six or seven moves out, never sure if your plans are going to unfold exactly as intended.

Lack of Mentorship

"When the student is ready, the teacher appears."

In order to find a mentor who can show you how to win at the political game without permanently losing your soul, you need to display (1) a desire to learn the perspective, (2) an innate ability to grasp and manipulate conceptual, abstract information, and (3) strength of character. If a mentor has not yet, to your knowledge, walked into your life, these are the areas to start working on.

Society Vilifies the Political Process

To learn anything, you must first let go of judgment. In a society that consistently decries anyone caught engaging in a political perspective, this is often hard to do with regard to that political perspective. Once someone concludes politics are evil, it can be extremely difficult for that person to allow himself later to come to a different conclusion.

I am fully aware that—even just from reading the title of this chapter—many readers will be skeptical, if not downright cynical, about anything I have to say here. You may love the idea of the Magic Moment. You may be reconsidering your relationships and your goals and applying the principles of active adaptation to them in order to engage more socially. But *politics?* I'm typing words here months before anyone will read them, and I can already feel the wariness.

People will talk themselves out of politics in many different ways: "I don't want to be like that," "My job doesn't offer me the flexibility to engage at that level," "I don't want to contribute to a toxic environment"—these are but a few of the rationalizations people use to opt out. In reality, none of these rationalizations hold water. No matter where you are or what you do, you are in a position to take full ownership over your career right now.

A Functional Perspective on Morality and Ethics

The concept of ethical politics is an oxymoron, which—not surprisingly—does not sit well with a lot of people. If you're going to win at politics, you're going to have to risk giving up control of your reputation to a certain degree . . . because your intended ethics are, in a way, irrelevant during the heat of battle.

The reality of the political fight is not what you intend but what others perceive. I may not *intend* to screw you over, but if that's what happens, I doubt very much you'll care about my intentions. And if I happen to have improved my situation at your expense, my apology will certainly ring hollow and my ethics will become suspect in your eyes. I can argue until I'm blue in the face that I meant no harm, but the fact remains: I improved my situation at your expense. When we bring in the outside arbiter, I'm going to have a tough time proving my ethical nature, aren't I, despite my good intentions?

When you're effective at changing the game, the person who was winning before you came along is going to call you a political snake. She won't see your ethics, she won't like you as a person, and she will be emotionally blind to how your mousetrap is better than hers. She will only see that you outmaneuvered her, and she will come to the same conclusion you would come to if the tables were reversed: that you're a political game player who is not to be trusted.

In your heart, you remain a principled individual—that is implied by the moral imperative. But people cannot see what is in your heart, only your action. On the one hand, they may see you refuse to engage for fear of making a mistake or being disliked, resulting in subjugation. On the other hand, they may see you engage, resulting in unflattering images being painted of you showing your "flexible" morality.

If you think you are a winner or could be a winner . . . if you want to not only keep your job but grow it . . . if you see a better future and want to make it manifest . . . then right now you must let go of the notion that there is some set of rules to be followed, or a referee who will award you a medal for playing the game the "right" way. There isn't. It is accepted that people will get hurt. It is also accepted that the game can be played by anyone, which means both good people and bad will take the field. Bad people fight dirty, fight for personal gain, and don't hesitate to exploit the weaknesses of others. And they stand between you and your goal. It's the world you were born into.

Practical Strategies for Introducing a Political Perspective

Now that we have an idea of what politics is about at a high level, let's break things down into more tangible, actionable strategies that you can use at work. The following five strategies can all be applied ethically, and under certain circumstances each will help ensure that everyone around you walks away from conversations with the same image in their heads. Not all of these strategies will work all the time, of course, nor will they all work for every individual. And to counterbalance the high-level, conceptual nature of the first part of this section, I have opted to present these strategies as tactically as possible, in the form of a little case study.

Ready?

Here's the situation: your boss is transferring to China at the end of the year, and there are two lead candidates to take her place—you and a peer of yours who we'll call . . . Shirky. Now Shirky's a little over his head already in his job, to the point where your team has been picking up his slack. You just learned through the grapevine that Shirky's been insinuating to upper management that *his* team has been carrying *you*. Clearly he's positioning himself for that promotion, and you put two and two together and determine that if Shirky gets the job, his first act will be to demote you in an attempt to either control you or push you out of the organization. It's a bad economy, you love your job, and you would not be able to easily replace it . . . at least not without uprooting yourself, which would not be so easy for you—you have older parents for whom you are the primary caretaker. So you make a decision. *Me and Shirky? We're not friends. My next Magic Moment will be when I get that promotion myself.*

The Functional and Social Perspectives Fail to Solve This Problem

You could go running to your boss—or your boss's boss—to complain about Shirky's scheming. It would probably be an easy conversation. You'd lay out the facts, your boss's boss would listen, thank you for sharing, and you'd leave.

But then what?

The person you just spoke to would make some calls, probably on the sly, to try to get some firsthand information about the situation. One of those calls might even be to Shirky (or to a friend who could approach Shirky). And what story do you think Shirky would tell?

Maybe he'd say, "Aw, shucks, you caught me . . . you're right, I don't deserve the promotion." Right. The chances of that are about zero. Instead, Shirky tells an entirely different story, and now look what happens: your boss's boss has two people—who she knows are both vying for the same position—who clearly aren't playing nicely in the sandbox together and who can't solve their own problems without help from higher up.

Suddenly, you're like a kid in the backseat on a cross-country drive who just complained to Dad that your brother hit you . . . and you're about to hear the equivalent of "I don't care who started it, if you think you can handle this promotion, you need to show me you two can figure out how to end it!"

Real smooth. Now not only do you have the same problem with Shirky but the promotion is now in jeopardy, and worse, even though Shirky is the one playing games, you're the one management's disappointed in.

So much for the "just lay out the facts" approach.

Strategy #1: Imagine Not the Next Conversation but the Conversation After That

What you need to do is, when thinking about the conversation you want to have, continue to play out "what next" scenarios so you can see how the following conversations and actions cascade from there. If you can anticipate how things will play out and see it won't end well, avoid that path. Never engage in a conversation that will lead to a predictably bad conclusion! Change the way you approach the conversation—control the frame—in order to steer to a more positive outcome.

In this case, you might find that a better way to highlight the concern would be to ask for a bigger budget and more staff—a much bigger budget. Your boss will balk at the request and inevitably call you into her office to ask about it. Now, on the surface, it may appear that you have a problem, but what you really have is a forum in which to discuss, in a very matter-of-fact way, where your team is spending its hours. The process will naturally expose the ways in which you are covering Shirky's behind.

This conversation leads to a very different "what then" series of actions. Now your boss's boss calls Shirky, but this time it's not a sly conversation to figure out what's up; it's to ask Shirky point-blank why so many of your guys are helping him out. From here, the options fork: either Shirky has a good answer, or he doesn't. If he doesn't, that's it, game over, you win. If he does, you and Shirky may get called together into your boss's boss's office, but if you do, that's OK, because now Shirky's on the defensive. In that follow-up conversation, you're a problem solver, not a complainer, and you can offer up any solution you want: give me additional budget, have Shirky report to me, split my team and give these guys to Shirky (and let management see your guys moan and complain about going from a good boss to a bad one) . . . it doesn't matter. After that session, your boss's boss will consider what just happened, conclude that you just made a play for the soon-to-be-open job, and appreciate the fact that you did it by stepping up. The fact that you played hardball will not be held against you, since you did it appropriately to put the screws to a non-performer. You win.

Strategy #2: Develop a Longer Time Horizon

You invite your boss's boss to lunch, at which you say, "Listen, I like this company. A lot. You've been good to me, and I see a path here for myself. I come to work every day trying to earn my position here by building a great team, growing my territory, achieving better results. I don't want to get locked into short-term thinking about the *next* promotion—I want to spend a few minutes with you talking about the bigger picture." If asked about the genesis for the conversation, you can respond honestly. "Look, we're like any team. Sometimes we're great, other times it gets tough. Right now, I can tell Shirky's feeling the heat from this horse race we're in, and if I'm seeing it in him, my guess is he sees it in me, too. I need a perspective check so I can stay above the fray and keep focused on what's important for the business." You just focused your boss's boss on your maturity, growth orientation, and proactivity. You've not only increased your chances for getting the job, but you're about to get a trove of information related to how to expedite the rest of your career (functional win), plus you just made a friend (social win).

Awesome.

Strategy #3: Love Thy Frenemies

"Shirky! Wassup! Listen, buddy, I owe you a thank you! Word on the street is that I've got a blind spot the size of a school bus and that you've been helping cover for me. I can't tell you how much I appreciate that—especially with you and me in this sort-of horserace for our boss's spot—and seriously, I don't even feel the slightest competition with you—it's just very cool that even with everything going on, you'd go the extra mile to help a friend. . . . I'm working to get my house in order now. . . . I'd feel awful if you didn't get the promotion because you were spread so thin covering for me. Any suggestions you have for me at all would be much, much appreciated!" Pause. Listen carefully, you just might hear Shirky crap his pants.

Note that not everyone can pull off using this approach. You need to be able to have fun with this one for it to work—and you have to be able to show genuine gratitude. The assumption here is that Shirky is telling the truth, and that your take on the situation has a hole in it somewhere. If you don't think you've missed anything and you really think Shirky's being a player, don't attempt this—you'll sound phony and amateurish, and if Shirky—who might be a better politician than you, we don't know—responds to you with "Knock it off, you and I both know that whole thing is a load of garbage. I don't know what your problem is or why you feel this need to attack me, but if that's the way you want to play it, game on," then you had better be prepared to use every weapon in your arsenal on him, because you're in a war.

Strategy #4: Change the Destination by Shaping the Journey

It's kind of hard to get from Chicago to Hawaii by bus. By the same logic, it's going to be pretty tough for Shirky to hit his numbers when you pull your team off his projects.

Politicians win fights by controlling resources. So control them. Shape the journey.

Strategy #5: Direct Offense

You call Shirky: "Shirky, what's this I'm hearing about you telling people you're covering for me?" You listen; you might learn something about a blind spot that you have. Assuming you don't hear anything surprising, you have two choices. You can either make a threat or take action. The threat, if you make it, needs to be specific, credible, implied, and provide Shirky with a clear path to avoid it. It may sound something like this: "Shirky, your numbers depend on my continued support of your efforts. Seventy-three percent of your revenue shows up on my P&L as internally supported projects. I have a headcount of three devoted exclusively to supporting your clients. And if you look at your own cost of goods sold, you'll see a line item for where you went over and above your allocated support dollars last year. I'm the one who supported you, and I have the offset on my P&L to prove it. If you keep feeding the rumor mill, you're going to get hurt. Reality doesn't support what you're selling."

Normally, I don't advocate making threats like this. Most people don't know how to make them and wind up inviting conflict and gamesmanship. Threats are also risky, since you are revealing information about yourself that can be used by the other side. If you misestimate your power base, you may be cooking your own goose. Still, it's a strategy, and if you have the numbers on your side, the force of personality to make it believable, and the reputation to make it credible, then in certain circumstances it can work.

The other option is to take action. In this example, you can actually divert your team's resources away from supporting Shirky and track the degree to which performance suffers. This approach is even riskier than making the threat, since you will have taken action that had a negative impact on the company's performance—the opposite of what you're supposed to be doing—while doing nothing to provide your boss or your boss's boss with a way to interpret your actions. There are times when this approach is necessary, but be careful. To engage in this strategy, you need to know that the cost you incur by allowing performance to suffer is less than the cost of an inevitable political struggle . . . and that's a very difficult thing to know.

Political Solutions Are Necessary

Shirky holds a competing vision for where the company should be headed, and he's trying to shape your journey by controlling the frame through which others view both your work and his. Since he's your peer, you have no authority over him.

Your boss, who's leaving, may or may not care to help you. And your boss's boss may not want to pick sides if she views Shirky's and your squabble as an interpersonal problem.

Which is why you need the strategies laid out above. Political solutions help you fight for control of the frame when you lack formal authority and when the stakes are too high to rely on your lovability.

No use complaining about it; it is what it is.

Summary of the Only Rule About Politics

Politics is basically what happens when the teacher leaves the room. Or when a group of adults try to govern themselves. When you like the direction things are heading, you tell everybody to play by the rules. When you don't like the direction things are heading, you change the rules. Or change the game. If you like the direction things are heading and someone else starts changing the rules in order to pull people in a new direction, you call him a politician. You attack his credibility. When you don't like the direction things are going and you're being ineffective at changing the rules, you attack the character of those setting the direction.

Again, I don't advocate becoming a game player, but it's naive to ignore the reality of how politics work. This whole thing about politics is a true prisoner's dilemma, in which a utopian, politics-free society is possible only if everybody agrees to play by the same rules, despite a strong incentive to cheat once everyone else has agreed to abide by the rules. So until human nature is perfected, career staying power will require an awareness of how to excel in the current, imperfect environment. If you want to win, you need to win *at every level*. You need to be politically strong, socially connected, and functionally superior.

When you operate at the political level, with your soul hanging from a peg waiting to be reclaimed, fighting for control of the frame, there is only one rule that you must, must, always, always bear in mind: the moral imperative.

The winner of the political battle gets to write the history, so by the nature of the beast, what's "ethical" and "moral" is determined by the winner. If you believe in your ethics and morality, then you have a moral obligation to engage and win; that is the only way you can be sure you are taking 100 percent full responsibility for yourself and your career. You also have a moral obligation not to take advantage of the situation, not to lose your idealism, and not to accept personal gain at the expense of the good of the whole.

It is not an easy balance to maintain, but it is necessary to walk that line if you are to build a career with staying power.

WHAT YOU LEARNED

▶ **What is politics?** *Politics is the process of framing issues to make people perceive them in a particular light. The functional perspective is concerned with the work itself; the social perspective is concerned with how that work gets done.*

The political perspective shapes both by dictating the frame through which functional and social work occurs. Engaging politically—controlling the frame—is the act of taking 100 percent personal responsibility for success and leaving nothing either to chance or to the whim of others.

► **What is the moral imperative?** *Politics are never to be used as a substitute for good work.*

► **What is the central trade-off demanded by the political perspective that makes it so difficult?** *Imagine running for office against a dirty incumbent. Your choice is to run an honorable campaign that will lose—and thereby subject yourself to a corrupt government—or run a dirty campaign and fight for the chance to wield power more honorably. The paradox of having to "put your soul in hock" for a chance at victory creates a very real, very tough moral dilemma: is it better to risk sacrificing your morality in order to save it, or to willingly submit yourself to the control of others?*

► **Is there a consequence if I do not engage in politics?** *Yes. By choosing not to engage, you forfeit some measure of control over your career and yourself.*

► **What if this topic makes me uncomfortable?** *What makes many people uncomfortable isn't politics per se but the idea of admitting to their own imperfect human nature. Hopefully, recognizing the inherent moral dilemma about engaging in politics will take some of the stigma of that away—or will at least challenge the idea that choosing not to engage is without consequence. If you struggle with this, congratulations, you're a human being.*

► **What five strategies can I use to control the frame more effectively?** *(1) Imagine the conversation after the next one. (2) Develop a longer time horizon. (3) Love thy frenemies. (4) Change the destination by shaping the journey. (5) Engage in direct offense.*

► **Politics seems relative. Are there any certainties about it?** *Yes, five. (1) You can no more avoid politics than you can avoid*

*love, hate, surprise, boredom, friendship, loneliness, frustration
. . . or deep personal contentment. Politics is a reflection of our
imperfect human nature. (2) When operating at the political
level, you can see both the best and the worst mankind has
to offer. (3) People will get hurt. When you decide to fight for
control of the frame, you take responsibility for that. Expect
to carry a knot in your stomach. (4) There are no rules. (5) You
cannot take 100 percent personal responsibility for your life
without engaging.*

Conclusion

Success comes in a variety of shapes and sizes. That's part of what makes life so exciting—you can know exactly where you're going and still not be able to anticipate all the twists and turns you'll need to take to get there. It's only when you get to the end and look back, with the power of hindsight, that you get to see which small decisions turned out to be the big breaks. Success never quite comes at you the way you'd expect. It's always a bit of a surprise.

"Hold on, hold on, hold on! Jase, are you saying I'm turning myself inside out doing all this Magic Moment, 100 percent personal responsibility, political perspective, pocket of ignorance adaptation stuff, and you still can't tell me how this success thing is going to play out?!"

Chillax, I'm not saying that at all. I've told you exactly how it will play out: commit to your goal, take full—FULL!—responsibility for shaping an environment conducive to success, focus, demonstrate persistence. At all times, remain open to new perspectives: if your functional ability doesn't get you home, look at things socially and adjust the way you communicate; if that leaves you frustrated, consider a political perspective and how you might control the frame. All the while, continue to execute like mad. When you do all this, success comes. That's how it plays out. Only I don't know precisely *where* or *when* it'll play out. The details are a mystery.

"Oh. Does that mean that luck will play a role in the timing of all this?"

Sure. Maybe. No. Look, I don't know. I don't even know what luck is, to tell you the truth. Chance? A big karmic force that guides us in ways we can't understand? A cosmic manifestation of sheer willpower? It's hard to know. The thing is it doesn't matter. However it gets to your door, opportunity will find you, and when it starts knocking, it won't matter if it found you through chance or karma or your hard work . . . all that will matter is what you do with it.

To help you prepare for that moment, I have decided to jettison the typical conclusion format of most business books for a little mini case study. The conclusion is normally where an author tells you what he already told you. I'm going to do one better: I'm going to walk you through an exercise that will help you internalize what you just read and practice applying it. Following the exercise is a quick recap of key concepts. Warning: I did not make the case easy; this is no cake walk that will let you pretend to have learned this material by memorizing lists. You're going to have to think about these situations, and you'll likely have more success if you work through the case with a group of three to five peers.

Suggested answers can be found at http://jasonseiden.com/super stayingpower.

Courting Success Through Magic Moments: A Case in Building Long-Term Security Through Small Daily Improvements

You are a manager on a twelve-person Web design team. Up until a year ago, your group had been a stand-alone company based in Chicago called Grooveball Productions (GP). For nearly a decade, GP had been a struggling little design shop, limping along, building catalogs, brochure sites . . . whatever it could get. Then, about two years ago, your boss hired two people—yourself and a young designer named Davis—and everything changed. Straight out of college, Davis seemed to waste a lot of time goofing off online . . . but something from your six years in the industry told you not to brush Davis aside. Indeed, when you dug deeper and saw what he was doing and how he was using Facebook and Flickr and YouTube to stay connected with friends, you got an idea: help companies use social media to engage their customers in ongoing conversation!

Your idea was to pitch companies on a whole new approach to customer engagement. Gone would be the transmission-style marketing pitches; instead, they would be replaced by more integrated, less formal campaigns that invited true participation. You weren't sure the idea would fly—would brands open themselves up to unfettered conversation? How would the traditional publicity machine respond? (Coming from the publicity world yourself, you were pretty sure they'd fight back . . . and how.) Despite the risks, you presented your idea at a Monday morning staff meeting, had marketing collateral prepared by Friday, and by the following Friday, one of your sales teams had landed GP's first social media client. Six months later, GP was no longer a sleepy little shop—it had more work than it could handle and an ever-growing waiting list! Mark, the owner of the firm, opened talks with one of your larger competitors, Practical Online Solutions (POS), about handling overflow work. You continued to outsource work to smaller shops while talks with POS continued; then, after six months, Mark announced he had finally negotiated a deal.

The deal Mark closed, however, was not the work-for-hire arrangement everybody at GP expected. Mark had sold the company. You remember how ecstatic everyone was at first—"Now we have real jobs!" became the battle cry at the impromptu celebration that night at the bar downstairs from your loft office. Apparently, POS had been keeping an eye on GP, and it was impressed with the explosive growth the firm had started to experience. The sale worked for everyone: GP got security and the backing of a major company, and POS got a book of business it knew how to support and cross-sell into over time. Everybody was a winner. It was great.

For about a month.

That's when sales suddenly stopped. Not your sales—social media stayed hot—but sales across the board at POS. It turned out that their sales had been declining for some time, a story masked by some rapid acquisitions they had been making . . . not too unlike the deal they made with GP. For a few months, GP was largely spared from the lay-offs and downsizing that began occurring elsewhere in the firm, but eventually your team got caught up in the grinder, too.

The first thing to happen, about three months ago, was that POS bought out Mark. While not exactly a surprise move, the timing was rather abrupt, and the conditions of the deal made it impossible for Mark to talk to you about clients. This created a major headache: Mark had been a very hands-on leader, and the terms of his nondis-closure agreement left some significant gaps in your ability to cover client projects. You couldn't imagine what could have happened to make POS want to cut Mark out so suddenly, or be willing to assume that kind of risk with clients, and you did your fair share of wonder-ing, *what the hell were they thinking?*

The second thing that happened was that you were promoted to take Mark's job. Given the circumstances of the promotion, you were reluctant to take it. When you discovered that it come without a sal-ary adjustment, you called your new boss and turned it down. Your boss made it clear that turning down the job was not an option and that no one was really expecting you to step up that quickly, that it was more a matter of showing to clients that POS was transitioning away from Mark seamlessly. You knew you were being used but felt there was not much you could do. You told your boss you'd think about it, and before you got home he sent you an e-mail telling you he had procured funds to give you a raise to go along with the increased responsibilities. You managed a smile. *I guess I was negotiating,* you thought to yourself.

Not four days into your new job and your team felt the full brunt of POS's financial troubles: Davis, the one who helped launch GP into social media, and a recent hire were let go. Worse, they were replaced with POS employees from other, disappearing divisions who needed a place to land. You couldn't believe it! It was the ugli-est form of political gamesmanship, with your team—one of the only well-performing divisions in the whole company—gutted to make space for cronies who had dragged down their previous divisions and now would drag down yours. Nobody so much as called you to give you a warning about what was happening—you learned the same way everyone else did, from an "All Staff" e-mail sent by Davis: "I've been fired?!?! WTF!!! I guess we all know what POS really stands for now!!!" Davis's e-mail had gone to the entire POS staff, from the CEO on down, and you knew you'd probably hear about that, but at the time you were more interested in helping Davis.

Here was the guy responsible for GP's magic, past and present, and some random VP who's never met him calls him on the phone and tells him security will be at his desk in a minute to escort him out. You walked out with Davis and promised him to look into what was going on. You fumed, but not for long. Less than two weeks after Davis was let go, so was the VP and the two people he tried parking with your group.

(You never did find out what the story there was.)

You managed to hire Davis and your other employee back, but only just: a company-wide hiring freeze went into effect the same day Davis re-signed. That was six weeks ago. Meanwhile, as leader of your team, you've been scrambling to stay abreast of operations. With all the turmoil at POS, none of your clients has retained a POS account manager for more than four months. For your oldest and most important clients, this means they've had no fewer than three account reps introduce themselves over the past year. The layoffs and hiring freeze have affected your ability to staff projects, too; whatever the plan was when GP was acquired by POS, that plan is no more. You're back to being short-staffed. And of the people you've got, your best one, Davis, is also the greenest and most aggravated. The more you explore various accounts, the more you discover how much Mark was shouldering himself! Of the ten people on the team, you'd guess that three are high performers (including both yourself and Davis), four are average, and three are not up to scratch. The workload being what it was, Mark was using these last three as warm bodies, occasionally having them pitch in to do rote work, but generally, Mark seemed to have been doing the work of four people and just hadn't gotten around to replacing them with higher performers. Now you discover that in your attempts to delegate work evenly over the past

few months, you've been unintentionally punishing your top performers by shifting the extra work Mark had been doing to Davis and
his high-caliber peers. *Terrific, I'm saddled with dead weight and my
top performers are probably looking for jobs.* Under the circumstances,
who could blame them?

You recently read a book in which you learned about a concept
called Magic Moments. A Magic Moment is *a moment of deep, personal contentment brought about by the perfection of the moment itself.
Magic Moments can be created through a recipe of a tough, realistic
goal, an environment conducive to success, and a winner's attitude.* You
decide that if you can get your team to create some Magic Moments
under the current circumstances, you should be able to capture some
of the magic from the GP days and turn that into bottom-line results.
Who knows where POS is going, but GP still has a strong reputation
worth protecting!

POS's demise is having a draining, negative impact on your group.
Whatever happens to POS in the long haul, you believe in GP, you
believe in the GP team, and you want to see your group succeed. If
the place were to fall apart tomorrow, you want to make sure the GP
division would remain intact. Your first step is to close ranks around
the GP group and isolate it from the negativity and gamesmanship
exhibited elsewhere. Next, you want to turn the GP culture around,
all the while delivering top-caliber results to your clients.

It won't be easy, but it's important to you. Maybe it's the fact you
just turned thirty-four, but there's something inside you that is telling
you that another two-year job stint wouldn't help. You've got to stop
running away and start trying to make something work where you
are. Win or lose, you're starting right now.

Sunday

It's Sunday evening. As you look at your schedule for the upcoming
week, you start thinking about tomorrow's staff meeting, at which you
would like to achieve the following:

▶ Create a clear vision for the team that appeals to your high performers, engages their interest, and gets them to stop partaking in the negativity rampant in the rest of POS.

▶ Engage everyone in a conversation that helps you determine which environmental factors are most important for you to get ahead of right now, without turning the meeting into a gripe session (your shoulders sag just at the thought of this; POS is *such* a mess, you can't even imagine where your crew will start!).

▶ Show your appreciation for the hard work everyone is doing.

▶ Demonstrate your commitment to the group.

▶ Discuss ongoing business and new sales.

▶ Create an action list for the week for yourself and for the team.

You've never run a meeting like this and aren't sure quite how it's supposed to go. You decide, rather than just talk about Magic Moments, this meeting should be a Magic Moment. Time is precious; gimmicks are not an option. As it is, you will barely have a chance to get through your agenda.

What should you do? You look over your list and wonder: *Is this even the right agenda? Did I miss anything?*

Monday

After the staff meeting, you return to your office just in time to answer a call from an important client. The client launches into an angry tirade about how a torrent of customer complaints is now visible on their Facebook profile. After a brief discussion, the client admits that the product being discussed was faulty and that the real frustration they have is with their own legal department, which has been dragging its feet about green-lighting a manager to go online and respond to the charges. However, the problem has been exacerbated by the lack of a POS account manager to provide practical guidance. The client makes a sarcastic remark about how wonderful the POS/GP marriage was supposed to be, and you know there's 80 percent truth to the client's "joke." You check the client's information while you're on the phone, and you discover that the person assigned to the project from the GP team is one of your not-up-to-scratch employees and that the client's account manager has changed six—six!—times in the past year.

You have an upset customer who is talking poorly about POS/GP and its employees. You understand the client's frustration about the account manager, but it is also clear to you that the client is venting and that much of the emotion being aimed at POS is really "smoke from a different fire," specifically, frustrations about its internal legal team's foot-dragging. How do you turn this conversation around? You don't want to belittle the client's concerns, but neither are you sure you can offer the client very much in the way of a functional solution—you hesitate to replace the account manager with a different team member for a number of reasons, but you also hesitate to move the project to one of your top performers who is already overloaded.

You know you are likely going to disappoint this client in the short run; your hands are tied. But there is a long-term solution, if you can convince the client to stick with you as you figure it out. But how much should you share about your plans? And what, if anything, should you be focused on at the social level to build trust and alleviate the pressure you are feeling? Ask yourself what you think this client wants to hear—what type of message, what tone. Should you continue to have the conversation over the phone or suggest a switch to a different communication channel?

Eventually, you hang up the phone. To help you clear your head for a moment so you can think about how best to handle the situation, you take a walk down the hall for a cup of coffee . . . where you bump into the very account manager you had just been talking about. Casually, you let the account manager know that you received an unhappy phone call from a client. The manager does not engage. You offer a bit more information, saying, "Yeah, I guess they've been having issues, and with all the turnover in the account manager role, they don't know where to turn. . . ." Rather than responding with inquisitiveness or a desire to fix the situation, the account manager becomes defensive.

What a day.

Still thinking about the Magic Moment, and about how important it is for you to continue to get maximum effort from everyone who touches your team, how can you take advantage of the informal setting to enlist the help of this account manager—over whom you have no formal authority—and get her to want to rise to your challenge? Think fast: you need to take control of the frame quickly in order to dispel the manager's defensiveness!

Tuesday

You have a scheduled lunch meeting with Davis. You need to know where his head is at and whether or not rumors about him being a flight risk are true. You also want to gauge his commitment to the team. He's a rising star with real potential, and if he's as committed as you are, you'd like to start handing over more responsibility to him. You've seen behaviors from him that suggest commitment but also behaviors that make it seem as if he's checked out. You're acutely aware that the two of you were hired at the same time and that the same week you got promoted, he got terminated. Though his termination was brief, you were the one who brought him back, giving you significant power over him now on multiple levels. Once upon a time, you two had been peers, separated by a few years of age but that's it. Does any of this weigh on his mind? Can your position be used to your mutual advantage?

Describe the lunch. Where do you go? Do you make reservations or grab something casual? How much time do you set aside for chitchat? How do you broach the topic of his assumed dissatisfaction, if at all? With the whole surprise firing a few weeks back, and as a new manager yourself, you have little idea where this conversation will go, what Davis might be thinking, or how you should respond if he says he is seriously considering leaving. What topics do you prepare to discuss just in case? What if he says that he is indeed looking elsewhere? What should you be prepared to discuss or negotiate, if anything? More than anything, since you can't cement Davis's commitment to GP, you want to make sure that lunch reestablishes the bond between the two of you. Can you leverage the Magic Moment model to guide you in a simple conversation? And if so, how? What does the goal look like when the entire objective is just to have a good conversation?

Wednesday

It's time to engage the folks at corporate POS.

For a year, you've felt like a leaf being blown about on the breeze at POS. You'd like some clarity around the state of the company, how much GP is subsidizing money-losing operations elsewhere (you're finally in a position, formally and politically, to ask that question and expect an answer), and what you can expect from POS leadership in terms of support during the coming year. What you'd *really* like to know is whether they'd consider selling your division (or spinning it back out), and if so, at what price. And, though it's not as strategically important, if you could give Davis the satisfaction of knowing what that whole situation was about when he was let go, you'd love that information.

You look at the phone: who do you even call? Your title is Creative Director, Social Media Services. You report to the Vice President, New Media, Chicago. Do you call your boss? Or not? Your boss seemed pretty ineffectual at protecting your team from others' meddling—was that a one-time thing or indicative of a lack of political clout? POS is based in Chicago; should you call the managing partner of the Chicago office, whose offices are at corporate? Or should you go to the top of the chain and get the CEO on the line? Then you start thinking: *Would the CEO even know about GP?* Maybe you should call the CFO? the President? the Senior Vice President of HR? the General Counsel? You don't even know what some of these people do! You tentatively decide to start with the head of HR; you'd like to call the CEO, but you wonder if, because of the politics, it would be safer starting someplace else.

Your mind wanders; you're no longer sure who to call. You take out a sheet of paper and draw three columns, labeling them functional, social, and political. Across the top of the page, you write "What GP means to POS." You scratch out "GP" and write your own name in. Then you scratch out "POS" and write in the CEO's name. You realize you're going to have to do this exercise for each person you're thinking about calling, so to keep things manageable, you shorten your potential call list to the CEO, the head of HR, and the CFO. Time to fill in the columns! When you're done, decide who should you call, why, and how you should lead off the conversation.

Thursday

Thursday afternoons are team meetings. The purpose of these is to review how much of Monday's action list has been accomplished and to discuss new or unexpected challenges that have come up during the week. These meetings are typically difficult because usually about a third of the team joins in by phone from client sites.

How can you structure the call to facilitate a Magic Moment despite having a third of your group dial in by phone? Is this call a potential Magic Moment, or should it be part of the feedback mechanism to set up a Magic Moment on the following Monday?

Friday

GP's biggest and oldest client calls . . . and wants out. Inconsistent performance from GP, unresponsiveness from the POS account manager, delayed program launches, lack of quantifiable results . . . you hear all of it. Then the client says something that makes you downright angry. She says, "I've told this to several people at POS and haven't heard from you or anyone else in two weeks. I'm done!"

On a personal level, a fire burns within you: you refuse to lose your biggest client the same week you decided to commit to restoring GP to its former glory! You need to do three things ASAP: First, you need to figure out where the opportunity is with this client, immediately. What do you think the client's most pressing issue is? Is it a question of goals? Environment? How long will it take to restore the client's faith and confidence in GP, and under what circumstances? How should you approach the client: functionally, socially, or politically? Second, you need to figure out how to engage your team to help fix the client's problems despite their workload. And finally, how can you use this situation to force the issue with POS? You got the CEO on the phone the other day just long enough to set up a breakfast meeting next week; this client could be your chance to make some demands that will put you back on a path to re-creating the old GP—either as part of the POS family or not. What will you say to the client? To your team? To the CEO?

Share Your Answers!

In each situation, I've tried to provide just enough structure to start you thinking one way or the other, and that's all. Share your suggested solutions online at http://jasonseiden.com/superstayingpower. While you are there, read how others approached the issue and see my own take on these scenarios.

Review of the Magic Moments and Three Perspectives Frameworks

If you want to develop staying power in your career, you need to do two things:

1. Look for—and find—Magic Moments at work.
2. Use the Three Perspectives model to enable the creation of Magic Moments by putting you in control and eliminating fear.

Magic Moments

Magic Moments are moments of deep, personal contentment, brought about by the perfection of the moments themselves.

There are three ingredients in a Magic Moment: a goal, an environment, and your attitude. For a Magic Moment to be possible, goals must be real, tough, and feedbacking—that is, they must take you to the edge of your abilities in some way while providing you with the feedback you need to know whether you are moving toward or away from success. Goals also require your commitment. The environment must be conducive to success, providing a location that offers access to the people and resources you require. You will need to take personal responsibility for shaping your environment. Finally, a winner's attitude—focused, persistent, and open—is needed to unlock a Magic Moment.

Three Perspectives

Work can be viewed through three perspectives: functional, social, and political. The functional perspective is concerned with *what* work gets done and involves solutions that include working more / better / faster / smarter / harder. The social perspective is concerned with *how* work gets done and involves solutions that include a handshake. The political perspective is concerned with the *stage* on which the work gets done and involves solutions in which you control the frame—that is, you dictate to others how you want them to interpret the facts of a given situation. Being able to adapt your perspective gives you an added measure of control when situations seem to get out of hand, allowing you to keep fear at bay and continue to create Magic Moments in a complex, ambiguous, and networked world.

Because where there are Magic Moments, there is resilience.

And where there is resilience, there is staying power.

Index